Venturing To Do Justice

venturing to do Justice

REFORMING PRIVATE LAW

by Robert E. Keeton

1969: HARVARD UNIVERSITY PRESS

CAMBRIDGE, MASSACHUSETTS

Preface

*A*CCELERATION OF private law reform has become an established fact. Changes introduced during the ten years commencing in 1958 were substantial and significant even when viewed one by one. A more comprehensive perspective discloses stunning departures from tradition. Most of the changes of substantive law were long-needed reforms. They continue to provoke controversy, nevertheless. Even more controversial, perhaps, are the methods by which these changes were accomplished. They present basic problems of legal process as well as substantive law.

To serve its highest aims, a legal system must have the stability and predictability essential to security, order, and evenhanded justice. If it is to continue even for generations, and the more clearly if it is to survive still longer, it must also have flexibility to change and ability to grow with the institutions and society it serves—the capacity, in short, to renew itself. Reconciling these competing demands for continuity and creativity is a central, perennial problem of legal order.

Law reform is the focus of this book. More particularly, the focus is reform of those areas of the law commonly referred to as private law—that is, the branches of law especially concerned with rights and duties of private individuals toward each other, enforceable through civil proceedings. Reflecting my bias and the limitations of my experience, most illustrations are drawn from tort law, though my purpose is to develop ideas of more general application.

The inquiry extends to institutional roles as well as substantive principles of private law reform—to processes as well as issues. Part One of the book is primarily concerned with processes of reform; Part Two, with principles of substantive law in two major areas deeply affected by the new spirit of change—the law applying to injuries caused by defective products and that applying to injuries caused by motoring. Part Three sketches a course for the future.

I gratefully acknowledge my debt to others who have written on this subject and to my colleagues, students, and friends who have contributed to the ideas expressed in this book. Among those to whom I am especially indebted are the late Professor Warren A. Seavey of Harvard and my brother, Dean Page Keeton of the University of Texas School of Law (the two persons with whom I have long been associated, always to my great benefit, in editing a casebook in torts); Professors Harold Berman, David Cavers, Lon Fuller, Louis Jaffe, John Mansfield, and Albert Sacks (colleagues at Harvard, each of whom has been a most helpful critic of parts of the manuscript for this book or articles that preceded it); Professor Jeffrey O'Connell of the University of Illinois College of Law (my collaborator in developing the Basic Protection plan and related ideas expressed in parts of Chapters 8 and 9); and Professors Leon Green, Robert Leflar, and Clarence Morris (my colleagues on the faculty of the Workshop for Torts Teachers at New York University in 1960, during which discussions occurred that led to the formulation of much that is expressed in Chapters 4 and 5).

I am grateful to Professor O'Connell and our publishers, Little, Brown and Co. and Dow Jones–Irwin, Inc., for permission, in writing Chapter 8 and parts of Chapter 9, to draw freely upon the product of our joint efforts, published in *Basic Protection for the Traffic Victim—A Blueprint for Reforming Automobile Insurance* (1965) and *After Cars Crash—The Need for Legal and Insurance Reform* (1967).

I gratefully acknowledge, also, the generous permission of the editors of the *Harvard Law Review*, the *Texas Law Review*, and the *Virginia Law Review* to use freely, and in many passages in exactly or virtually the form of initial publication, materials from my: "Conditional Fault in the Law of Torts," 72 *Harv. L. Rev.* 401 (1959); "Creative Continuity in the Law of Torts," 75 *Harv. L. Rev.* 463 (1962); "Judicial Law Reform: A Perspective on the Performance of Appellate Courts," 44 *Tex. L. Rev.* 1254 (1966); "Is There a Place for Negligence in Modern Tort Law?" 53 *Va. L. Rev.* 886 (1967). I have drawn heavily on the first of these articles in writing parts of Chapters 7 and 9 of this book, on the second in writing parts of Chapters 4 and 5, on the third in writing parts of Chapters 1, 2, and 3, and on the fourth in writing parts of Chapter 9.

Finally, I express my gratitude to Roger Henderson, Teaching Fellow at Harvard Law School, 1967–69, for his reliable and thoughtful research assistance, and to Mrs. Maria Baldi Hooks for her patient and proficient secretarial services in the preparation of the manuscript.

September 1968

Contents

One

Changing Processes of Law Reform

For full titles of journals cited see A *Uniform System of Citations*, published by the Harvard Law Review Association.

Chapter 1

Courts and Legislatures as Agencies of Abrupt Change

*T*HE MOST striking impression that results from reading the weekly outpouring of torts opinions handed down by appellate courts across the nation for the decade commencing in 1958 is one of candid, openly acknowledged, abrupt change.

If the validity of this assertion seems doubtful to some, perhaps the explanation lies not in fundamental disagreement about the performance of appellate courts during this period but in a difference of perspective from which that performance is viewed. Advocates and judges in many states, from their point of view as professionals in the appellate arena, may observe that their own appellate courts did not actively participate in this decade of accelerating change. They may rightly say, for example, that the participating courts numbered barely more than half of the state courts of last resort, and that those participating with more than a single overruling decision were a minority. Even in a court that was very active in this process of change, it may be said, relatively few opinions overruled precedents and openly changed the law of the state.

Take another perspective for a time, however—that of an outside observer seeking to find what is distinctive about judicial performance in appellate courts during the decade commencing in 1958 as compared with that during other periods of equal length. In that focus the most striking thing one sees is change, and change extending not merely to the law itself but also to the processes of changing law.

Other official bodies empowered to effect law reform—legislatures, juries, and administrative agencies—continued to act in more familiar and accustomed ways. They were not supplanted or even limited as instrumentalities of law reform. Courts, then, did not occupy the field or fulfill the total need. Nor, on the other hand, did the spirit of reform underlying the distinctive record of appellate courts during this decade produce a corresponding increase in the reform-mindedness of juries, administrative agencies, and legislatures.

As important and interesting as particular reforms of substantive law achieved during this period may be, they are less significant in the long run than changes that occurred in processes and attitudes. These were perhaps more subtle than doctrinal innovations but there is no lack of evidence that they occurred. A catalog of reforms in tort law accomplished during this period will indicate not only the scope of change in substantive law but also a remarkable shift in the attitudes of appellate judges toward law reform.

During the decade commencing in 1958, various state courts of last resort handed down decisions candidly and explicitly overruling precedents on a wide range of problems in the law of torts.[1]

A large number of these overruling decisions eliminated or narrowed the scope of immunities that had shielded government units and charitable organizations from ordinary liability for injuries negligently caused to others. In a more controversial area of immunity, a few decisions abrogated rules barring suits by family members against each other; under the new doctrine, for example, a child injured in an automobile accident caused by his parent's negligent driving is allowed to recover damages from the parent (or, to be realistic, from the parent's liability insurance company).

Another group of decisions overturned older rules that had placed special obstacles in the way of recovering damages for negligently inflicted mental suffering.

A considerable number of courts during this period overturned precedents in order to allow suit on behalf of a child for injury sustained from a negligently caused prenatal impact—for example, injury to the child in the mother's womb when the mother was in an automobile accident negligently caused by another person.

Another special rule, abrogated in a few decisions during this period, had barred a wife from recovering against a negligent third person for her loss of consortium resulting from injury to her husband. It is a defensible view, perhaps, that only the injured spouse should have a cause of action and that the change needed, in states where the husband but not the wife has been allowed to recover for loss of consortium, was to deny this right to the husband rather than to grant the wife a similar right. In any event, this anachronistic discrimination against women has few defenders save on the ground that the respon-

---

[1] The overruling decisions referred to in the text paragraphs that follow are collected in the Appendix.

sibility for considering the change is that of legislatures, not courts.

Under the decisional law of England, transported to America, death of either the wrongdoer or the victim terminated liability for injuries negligently caused. This plainly unfair rule has been modified by statutes in England and America. Most jurisdictions have two types of statutes. One type, called wrongful death acts, allows survivors to recover for their resulting losses. The other, called survival acts, allows the successors in interest of the deceased, who frequently are exactly the same group of survivors, to recover damages for losses and pain and suffering incurred by the deceased during any period he lived after the injury. In general, the wrongful death acts have long been interpreted as allowing only for tangible losses such as loss of money and services the deceased would have contributed to the survivors. Among the tide of overruling decisions during the period under discussion were some that reinterpreted death and survival acts. Several of these decisions allow a broader measure of damages under death acts. These decisions were reached even though, as we shall see in Chapter 6, a court's overruling its former interpretation of a statute is even more controversial than overruling its pure case-law precedents.

Common law decisions developed an inequitable set of rules regarding the allocation of legal responsibility in cases of injuries to which misconduct of several persons contributed. A pair of rules disallowed apportionment of damages among two or more defendants whose conduct contributed to injuring an innocent plaintiff. One rule made each such defendant liable to the plaintiff for full damages (though the plaintiff could collect his full damages only once). The second rule denied contribution among the wrongdoers, with the result that when the plaintiff collected fully against one, the other paid none of the loss. A few court decisions of the period in question abrogated one or the other of these rules, or abrogated related rules bearing upon the effect of a plaintiff's accepting a partial payment in settlement with one of the wrongdoers—for example, a rule discharging a plastic surgeon from liability for carelessly aggravating the injuries caused by the wrongdoer with whom the plaintiff settled, even though the settling parties intended that their agreement not discharge the surgeon.

One of the most frequently applicable of the inequitable common law rules for cases involving misconduct of more than one person is the rule that a contributorily negligent person is completely barred from recovering anything from another person whose negligence also contributed to his injury, even though the other was far more negligent than the injured person. Many state legislatures have modified this rule by comparative negligence statutes providing for apportionment of damages (that is, allowing the plaintiff to recover some damages but not as much as an innocent victim could have recovered). Most of these statutes apply only to special types of cases (for example, claims against railroads growing out of crossing accidents); only a few legislatures have adopted comparative negligence statutes of general application.

In 1967 an intermediate appellate court in Illinois, invited by the Supreme Court of the state to reconsider the contributory negligence rule on the merits, decided in favor of abrogating it and adopting a form of comparative negligence. However, when the matter came before the Supreme Court of Illinois for full hearing on appeal, in 1968, a majority of that court concluded that if this controversial change is to be made, it should be made by the legislature, not by the courts.

In some circumstances the rule barring recovery on the theory of contributory negligence has been extended to what is called imputed contributory negligence. For instance, an employer who suffers bodily injuries while a passenger in a truck negligently driven by his employee may be barred from recovering damages from the negligent driver of the other vehicle with which the truck collided; the employee's negligence may be imputed to the employer. Imputed contributory negligence rules have been under attack, and a few abrogating decisions were handed down during the period under discussion.

Contributory negligence rules have produced special stress when applied to injuries to children. One decision overturned earlier rules with respect to presumptions about the capacity of children of specified ages to be contributorily negligent.

Another overruling decision somewhat expanded the scope of a railroad company's duty with respect to hazards at grade crossings.

Owners and occupiers of land were especially favored by the common law. They had the benefit of legal rules that defined very narrowly their duties to others on their premises. These rules have long been under attack, and during the decade beginning in 1958 a number of decisions abrogated precedents and moved nearer to imposing as full responsibility on this group as is imposed on persons generally for injuries they negligently cause. Among these were decisions increasing the landlord's potential liability to persons on the premises with the tenant's consent and increasing the occupier's potential liability to firemen and to trespassing children.

Somewhat analogous to the special shield the common law provided for owners and occupiers of land is a rule protecting a host driver from liability to his guest passenger for injuries caused by ordinary negligence, as distinguished from gross negligence or worse. In most states this rule was adopted by the legislature in a guest statute, passed under the influence mainly of two ideas—one, that only an ingrate would sue his host and, two, that allowing suits by guests against host drivers who have liability insurance would open the door wide to collusive claims. In a few states, the rule disfavoring guests was developed by decisions rather than by statutes. In two such states—New Jersey and Wisconsin —older decisional rules favoring drivers and disfavoring guests were abrogated by court decisions of the early 1960's.

Another decision in Wisconsin abrogated an earlier rule that distinguished between gross negligence and ordinary negligence, holding instead that all forms of negligence should be considered under the framework of the Wisconsin comparative negligence statute, which allows damages to be apportioned according to degrees of fault.

Closely related were decisions in Wisconsin and elsewhere abrogating a doctrine of assumption of risk under which, for example, a guest passenger in a car might be barred because he voluntarily encountered a known risk in riding with a driver he knew to be unfit, even though the guest had such good reason for accepting the ride that he was not negligent in doing so.

The Kentucky court overruled a line of decisions establishing a doctrine sometimes referred to as the Kentucky streetcar rule, under which the streetcar company was liable for damage done when a streetcar left its tracks and entered the private property of an abutting owner, even though the accident happened without any negligence. By analogy, perhaps, any motorist would likewise be liable for damage done when his car left the highway without his fault. Under the new rule, fault must be shown to establish liability in this kind of situation.

On what has become for torts lawyers a notable day in July 1863 a barrel of flour fell out of a second-story window above a shop on an English street, striking and injuring a pedestrian. He could not prove

7

who caused the barrel to fall, or how, but the court allowed him to recover, Chief Baron Pollock remarking: "Res ipsa loquitur." [2] This was the origin of a doctrine allowing recovery without specific proof of fault when the plaintiff can show an incident that "itself speaks" fault.

There has been much controversy about the technical requirements and the legal effect of this doctrine. One of the overruling decisions in the decade beginning in 1958 abrogated a rule that the doctrine gives rise to a presumption, conclusively establishing negligence, rather than an inference, which jurors might find to be outweighed by other evidence. Another overruling decision permitted application of this doctrine in a limited type of malpractice cases against doctors, thereby avoiding the usual requirement that such a claim be supported by the testimony of a qualified physician willing to say that in his opinion the defendant physician deviated in some way from professional standards.

Another overruling decision bearing on methods of proving negligence concerned a rather technical problem regarding the effect to be given, in a tort case, to proof that the conduct of one of the parties to an accident was in violation of some criminal statute.

One of the perennial controversies in tort law concerns the extent of liability for negligence. It is generally agreed that one should not be held liable, down through eternity, for everything to which his careless act may eventually contribute. For example, suppose a building owner carelessly allows the modern equivalent of a barrel of flour to fall from his window and strike a pedestrian who is on his way to catch a scheduled airline flight, that the pedestrian is delayed for first aid and takes a later flight, and that he is killed when the later flight crashes. The building owner is not liable for the death; his negligence was not a legal cause of that event, even though it may have been one among the many antecedents we might refer to as causes in fact.

Few would disagree about this case. But it is easy to imagine tougher cases. For example, should a bank that negligently dishonors its depositor's check be liable for the arrest of the depositor on charges of passing a bad check? One decision of the period in question overturned a precedent that had favored banks in this kind of case. Another overruling decision, of highly debatable validity, rejected precedents that had favored a rule of legal cause defining the scope of liability according to foreseeable risk; the court reinstated still older precedents

[2] Byrne v. Boadle, 2 H. & C. 722, 159 Eng. Rep. 299 (1863).

under which a decision turns on whether or not the plaintiff's injury was a "natural and proximate" result of the defendant's negligence.

"Caveat emptor"—let the buyer beware—is a fair enough characterization of much of the law applicable to bargaining. Apart from contract remedies, tort law sometimes protects the victims of misrepresentation by allowing an action for damages for deceit. But the scope of freedom for "seller's talk" that nobody is supposed to take seriously remains broad. An overruling decision by the Massachusetts court in 1952 narrowed this freedom slightly by holding that a lessor is subject to legal responsibility for falsely stating to a prospective tenant that a third person has made a specific offer for the lease. During the decade under consideration, other decisions have moved in this direction, but without finding it necessary to overrule precedents explicitly.

Another kind of case in which contract and tort theories have interacted concerns liabilities for injuries caused by defects in products or structures. The common law of torts developed a privity requirement, under which the injured person was denied recovery against one whose negligence was responsible for a defect if there was no privity between them—no special relation, such as a contractual relation. A process of erosion of this harsh rule by exceptions and qualifications has long been under way. In the period under discussion a number of decisions directly overruled precedents and discarded the privity requirement.

Even more significant has been a shift toward strict liability for harms caused by defective products—that is, liability based on a showing that a defect in the product caused plaintiff's injury, and without any showing that the defect came about because of the defendant's negligence. Overruling decisions in the 1960's have contributed to this shift. In view of the number of states making the shift, its impact on tort theory, and its bearing upon processes of private law reform, this is perhaps the most important of the many areas of overruling decisions during the decade commencing in 1958.

There were overruling decisions also on questions of procedure having substantial impact on the trial of tort cases. These concerned per diem arguments (for example, assigning a stated number of dollars per day for pain and suffering and calculating on a blackboard, in the presence of the jury, how much this amounts to for the period of predicted duration of the pain); other methods of advocacy related to per diem arguments; instructions to the jury on unavoidable accident; an outmoded rule that sometimes a party moving for a directed verdict thereby impliedly waives jury trial; qualification of a medical witness; interpreting limitation statutes so as to give effect to an "opportunity to know" rather than an "absolute repose" standard in malpractice cases involving such things as leaving a sponge or a surgical needle in the patient's abdomen; and the standard for determining whether a verdict should be directed.

This catalog, comprehensive but not exhaustive, covers more than ninety overruling decisions on at least thirty-five topics, even if immunities and strict products liability are each counted as only one topic. These changes are significant in nature as well as in number. With perhaps a few exceptions they are regarded almost universally as much needed improvements of tort law.

Also significant is the scope of participation in this movement— participation by courts of last resort in just over half of the fifty states. A roll of the courts making notable early contributions to these changes must include California, Illinois, Michigan, New Jersey, New York, and Wisconsin. Courts of last resort in the following states contributed at least four such decisions: Kentucky, Minnesota, Oregon, Pennsylvania, Texas, and Washington. Other states whose courts of last resort each rendered at least one decision notable by this standard are widely scattered geographically and politically—including the New England states of Connecticut, Massachusetts, New Hampshire, and Rhode Island; the southern states of Mississippi, North Carolina, and Florida; the border states of Maryland and West Virginia; the midwestern states of Iowa, Ohio, and Nebraska; the western states of Colorado, Idaho, Montana, and Nevada; and in the far Pacific the two newest states of Alaska and Hawaii.

Courts that have rendered a single overruling decision in ten years, and perhaps with dissent even then, can hardly be regarded as venturesome. But the total array of these overruling decisions is nonetheless impressive, and the more so when compared with what courts of the same states had done in other periods of equal length.

This manifest sense of judicial responsibility for increased participation in reforming and improving decisional doctrines did not come to flower overnight. Rather the seeds were planted long before, and they were cultivated by at least a generation of somewhat lonely dissenters, both on the bench and in the law schools of the nation.

A change in the performance of appellate courts of this scope is, of course, controversial. Yet the case for courts' accepting more than their traditional share of responsibility for improving the law is very strong.

INSTITUTIONAL POWER AND RESPONSIBILITY
FOR PRIVATE LAW REFORM

To urge merely that courts have an important role in change as well as in constancy is to state nothing new. Judge Benjamin Cardozo [3] and Dean Roscoe Pound [4] expressed this idea cogently for their generation. And it is not peculiar to American jurisprudence. It underlies the whole Anglo-American tradition and can be found in other legal systems, though less prominently.[5] The idea inevitably emerges when professionals of the law pause to think seriously about their legal system. Indeed, it is indisputable that our legal tradition assigns to courts a creative role in improving law, as well as a guardian's role in preserving its continuity and predictability.

This is not to say that judicial performance either can be or should be a substitute for the law reform activity of persons in other positions, both official and unofficial. No institution or group in a democratic society has exclusive responsibility for private law improvement. The two institutions with primary responsibility are courts and legislatures, but even together they do not occupy the entire field.

Every democratic society has depended to some extent on ad hoc groups to initiate needed private law improvement. More often than not, a legislature has been the institution formally effecting change, but only a very incomplete view of the process of reform would overlook the roles of others in prodding the legislatures to act. The need for change itself sometimes stimulates the formation of a pressure group that commands a legislature's attention. Even when there is no natural grouping of persons to become an effective lobby, someone may appear to champion reform. Lawyers, individually and in groups, have been among those active in this way. For example, it has long been regarded as within the finest traditions of the profession for an advocate to battle vigorously and win for a client whose legal rights are founded on an unjust rule of private law and, after the judgment has become final, to work for legislative abrogation of the unjust rule.

The classic illustration comes from the life of Thomas Talfourd. "As a barrister Talfourd had successfully represented a father in a suit over the custody of a child. Judgment for Talfourd's client was based on his

[3] Benjamin Cardozo, *The Growth of the Law* (1924).
[4] Roscoe Pound, *Interpretations of Legal History* (1923), p. 1. See also Pound, *Jurisprudence* (1959), III, 560–566 (discussing creative judicial empiricism as a mode of growth of the law).
[5] See Pound, *Interpretations of Legal History*, pp. 1–21.

superior legal right, though the court recognized in the case at bar that the mother had a stronger moral claim to custody than the father. Having thus encountered in the course of his practice an injustice in the law as then applied by the courts, Talfourd later as a member of Parliament secured the enactment of a statute that would make impossible a repetition of the result his own advocacy had helped to bring about." [6]

Steps have been taken from time to time to institutionalize at least some limited roles of initiating private law improvement. One notable step of this kind was the creation of the American Law Institute (ALI), whose function was initially conceived as primarily one of stimulating and aiding the courts of the various states to develop decisional rules in a more orderly and consistent way.[7] Its early work was surely consistent with an assumption that in the main the law improvement it proposed would be accomplished by judicial decisions in cases of first impression, filling out the interstices of developed state law, rather than overturning decided rules either by statutes or by overruling decisions. However, after early concentration on the continuing development of incomplete court-made law, and to less extent upon improved rules of judicial procedure,[8] the ALI began to extend its concerns to statutory law as well.[9] In later years, increasing attention has been given to proposals for statutory reform, including such undertakings as the Model Penal Code, the Study of the Division of Jurisdiction Between State and Federal Courts, A Model Code of Pre-Arraignment Procedure, the Federal Estate and Gift Tax Project, and A Model Land Development Code.

Other institutions have been developed with a primary objective of statutory rather than decisional law improvement—including improvements of scope and nature such that the term "reform," with its stronger nuances, seems apt. Notable among such institutions are the Commissioners on Uniform State Laws [10] and state law revision com-

---

[6] Fuller and Randall, "Professional Responsibility: Report of the Joint Conference," 44 *A.B.A.J.* 1159, 1162 (1958). For a reference to Talfourd's two roles —as counsel for the morally undeserving father and thereafter sponsor of the corrective bill—see "The Infant Custody Bill," 21 *Law Magazine* 145, 152 (1839).

[7] 1 *ALI Proceedings* 12–18 (1923).

[8] "ALI Code of Criminal Procedure" (1930). For a later development in relation to evidence rules see "Model Code of Evidence" (1942).

[9] For example, Airflight Act (Tent. Draft No. 1, 1937); Property Act (Tent. Draft No. 1, 1937); Contribution Among Tort-Feasors Act (Tent. Draft No. 1, 1938).

[10] For a relatively early sketch of the history of the National Conference of Commissioners on Uniform State Laws, commencing with the first conference at

missions, of which that in New York was the first [11] and appears still to be the most active.[12]

Less formally organized but no less active in private law improvement have been reform-bent contributors to law journals and numerous law teachers, using not only journals but other channels of communication as well to convey their sense of the needs and the ways they could be met. For example, channels are sometimes opened because countless program planners for a wide variety of meetings, professional and otherwise, are constantly looking for controversial speakers.

To observe that there are severe limitations upon the effectiveness of all these various institutions, groups, and individuals is not to disparage their work. Their contributions have been significant indeed. But in final analysis their efforts are brought to fruition only through institutions with the power to accomplish private law reform. Of these, a small role is assigned to institutions such as administrative agencies, but the power to take the formal step necessary to effect change in private law is mainly in the courts and legislatures. Thus, even when considering potentially enlarged roles for the outside initiators of law reform, we must be concerned with the distribution and effective use of power inside the courts and legislatures.

A tradition of law improvement by creative judicial action has been part of the common law system from a point as near its beginnings as a custom can be said to have become tradition. At the very beginning, necessarily a high percentage of the courts' creative contribution consisted of deciding cases of first impression. Today, however, most of the judiciary's work—perhaps even nine tenths of it as Cardozo suggested in an earlier generation [13]—is in the tradition of spinning out applications of accepted precedents and their far-reaching implications. And

---

Saratoga, August 24–26, 1892, see *Handbook of the National Conference of Commissioners on Uniform State Laws and Proceedings*, 37th Annual Meeting (1927), pp. 3–5.

[11] Law of May 16, 1934, ch. 597, § 1, [1934] N.Y. Laws 1289; now appearing with amendments as N.Y. Legis. Law § § 70–72 (McKinney 1952).

[12] See, for example, "Report of the Law Revision Commission, N.Y." (1963).

[13] *The Growth of the Law* (1924), p. 60. See also Clark and Trubek, "The Creative Role of the Judge: Restraint and Freedom in the Common Law Tradition," 71 *Yale L. J.* 255, 256 (1961); Friendly, "Reactions of a Lawyer—Newly Become Judge," 71 *Yale L. J.* 218, 222 (1961); Jones, "Law and Morality in the Perspective of Legal Realism," 61 *Colum. L. Rev.* 799, 803 (1961); Mishkin, "The Supreme Court 1964 Term—Foreword: The High Court, the Great Writ, and the Due Process of Time and Law," 79 *Harv. L. Rev.* 56, 60 (1965).

most of the remaining tenth or so of a court's output is well within "the leeways of precedent." [14]

Nonetheless, in the legal systems of American states it has long been assumed that one way a court may act creatively is to overrule its own precedents. The English tradition on overruling precedents has been quite different.

It may be said that English and American views, though evolving from a common source, took opposite turns in the nineteenth and early twentieth centuries—the English toward a more restrictive view that disallowed overruling and the American toward a broader view that expanded the legitimate grounds for overruling. Perhaps Pound's point of view toward overruling, plainly conservative in comparison with practices of American courts even before 1958, was nearer to the source idea than either the American or the English practice of the late nineteenth and early twentieth centuries. Pound supported the overruling of earlier decisions, in an Oregon case he cited,[15] as "squarely within Blackstone's proposition" justifying judicial rejection of a precedent that is "flatly absurd or unjust." [16] Even the more conservative view among American judges of the mid-twentieth century would allow for such things as these: on rare occasion changing a rule long questioned and only fluctuatingly applied; overruling a decision that is in irreconcilable conflict with another; changing a rule that has caused great confusion; and overruling when the court is convinced that the reason for the precedent no longer exists, that "modern circumstances and justice combine" to justify the change, and that "no one's present personal rights or vested property interests will be injured" by it.[17]

[14] Karl Llewellyn used the quoted phrase as a section title in *The Common Law Tradition—Deciding Appeals* (1960). Llewellyn's emphasis on interstitial creativity, however, may tend to understate the role of courts in accomplishing more abrupt change. See Clark and Trubek, "The Creative Role of the Judge." Perhaps the same is true of Cardozo's writings and of his judicial performance when judged, perhaps unfairly, by the standards of later generations rather than his own. For example, in MacPherson v. Buick Motor Co., 217 N.Y. 382, 111 N.E. 1050 (1916), his opinion proceeded not on the theory of overruling precedents but on the theory of explaining that all the seemingly isolated exceptions to a privity requirement were in fact expressions of a previously unstated principle that was made the basis of decision in the case sub judice. The dissenting opinion made clear that the newly formulated principle was bound to change the effect of many precedents. 217 N.Y. at 395–401, 111 N.E. at 1055–1057.

[15] State v. Mellenberger, 163 Ore. 233, 95 P.2d 709 (1939).

[16] Pound, *Jurisprudence* (1959), III, 565, citing Sir William Blackstone, *Commentaries*, I, *70.

[17] The quoted language is that of Chief Justice Bell, dissenting in Restifo v. McDonald, 426 Pa. 5, 14–16, 230 A.2d 199, 203–204 (1967).

In 1966, the contrast between American and English views about overruling was softened by the House of Lords' declaration that henceforth they might overrule their earlier decisions.[18] At present, then, both the American and the English legal systems acknowledge that their respective courts of last resort are empowered to overrule their own precedents. The very recognition of this power implies a corresponding responsibility to exercise it—albeit with restraint—when occasion demands.

Restraint in exercising the judicial power to overrule precedents is essential to the stability of law. Yet abstention from exercising this power defeats stability itself. A practice of consistently and rigidly adhering to precedent eventually produces an accumulation of outmoded rules. This truth is rarely challenged even by those who most vigorously oppose judicial overruling of precedents. They assert, however, that it is the province of the legislature, not the court, to meet the need for reform. For reasons to be suggested shortly, the assertion that legislatures could perform this task, if only they would, grows ever more questionable in our changing social and political order. Even if legislatures could do the task alone, moreover, their practice has conclusively demonstrated that they do not do it. If courts also fail to act when law reform is needed, the consequence will be a constantly increasing heritage of outmoded rules. Courts refusing to overrule precedents outright are virtually forced to accomplish reform by devising a labyrinth of rules with dubious and unpredictable implications. Thus overpowering demands of justice encourage such courts to make casuistic distinctions that produce doubt rather than certainty, irregularity rather than evenhandedness, and vacillation rather than constancy. Rigorous judicial abstention from overruling precedents defeats the very stability that those who embrace it are trying to preserve.[19]

[18] See the engaging report of the very restrictive English tradition and its demise in Leach, "Revisionism in the House of Lords: The Bastion of Rigid Stare Decisis Falls," 80 *Harv. L. Rev.* 797 (1967).

[19] Compare Bing v. Thunig, 2 N.Y.2d 656, 661, 143 N.E.2d 3, 5 (1957), wherein the court chose to overrule precedents recognizing immunity of a hospital rather than to rest the decision on the ground that negligence of the nurses in that case might be classified as "administrative" and not "medical." From prior decisions applying such a distinction, the court observed, "there is to be deduced neither guiding principle nor clear delineation of policy; they cannot help but cause confusion, cannot help but create doubt and uncertainty."

CHANGING FACTORS RELEVANT TO THE FREQUENCY OF OVERRULING PRECEDENTS

If courts are not to abstain from overruling precedents, what factors should determine the frequency and scope of the exercise of this undisputed power and responsibility?

Regardless of who is to accomplish the changes—courts or legislatures—the practice of breaking with precedent must be somewhat greater in a mature legal system than in one that is in the earlier stages of development.

Even after centuries of development of the Anglo-American legal tradition, as we have noted, decisions that resolve previously unsettled questions continue to be a vital part of the output of the courts. But as precedents continue to accumulate, the range for such interstitial creativity narrows. Correspondingly, the need for candid breaks with precedent increases, both because there are more decisional rules and because many of the rules are older and more likely to be outmoded.

We must then ask to what extent it is realistic to look to legislatures to reform the law. There was a time in American history when, not only in the settled agricultural communities at the geographical and social center of the country, but also in both the frontier West and the industrialized East, men were less hurried and harried than today. There were fewer problems to solve and more time to solve them—or to fail in the effort. The sessions of a legislature in the past could at least seriously consider proposals for law reform.

It may be said that institutions for initiating private law reform, nonexistent in those earlier days, have sprung up and become increasingly active during the twentieth century. But, as we have noted, their work comes to fruition mainly through action of legislatures or courts. If a legislature is to act on a proposal generated by a law institute or a law revision commission, it still must take the time for deliberations on the proposal.

The legislatures of the present day do not approach those of fifty years ago in their capacity to make considered decisions on proposals for law reform, wherever the proposals may have originated. Today, in state after state, the reported experience of those close to the legislative process is that inertia and lack of time are major factors determining what bills are enacted and what bills fall by the wayside. In some states, legislative rules require that every bill be reported out of committee before a session ends, and the drive for adjournment produces a flood of committee recommendations against passage—if for no other reason than that there has not been time to study the bills as carefully as prudence demands before enactment can be recommended. In other states, bills may die in committee. A legislator's personal privilege to call a limited number of bills out of committee to the floor for action is usually a treasured right to be expended only for purposes that count most by his standards; one can hardly be surprised that these standards seldom give high priority to bills proposing to modernize outmoded decisional rules of law.

That so few law reform bills are passed is not a weakness to be charged against legislators. Rather, it is an institutional limitation to be taken into account when we attempt to appraise realistically the potentiality for law reform of a modern state legislature. Only the most compelling needs are likely to capture its attention. In these circumstances, the aphorism that a legislature's failure to enact a change is an expression of approval of the law as it stands is a patent fallacy. Year after year the legislators fail to act on proposals for reform concerning which the majority of them individually have no view. Among these, no doubt, are proposals they would favor if their time and attention could be devoted to reaching considered judgments on the merits.

We cannot expect any improvement in this respect. In view of the continuing rise of other demands upon the legislator's limited time and energies, we must expect that the inherent institutional limitations upon the potentiality of state legislatures for reforming the law will be manifested even more severely in the future.

Perhaps no one has ever doubted that changing times require changes in the substantive law that governs men's relations. Law must be contemporary to be viable. Yet, strangely, it is often assumed that the respective roles of courts and legislatures in effecting these substantive changes should remain immutable. Here, as in the case of substantive law, change is inevitable, and attempts to deny change altogether will be self-defeating. Thus, in light of the combination of increased needs and increased institutional limitations upon the potentiality of legislatures for reforming law, courts and legislatures that today confine themselves to methods of law reform appropriate for earlier days will fail to discharge their current responsibilities.

Underlying the historic allocation of power and responsibility for law reform is a principle that responsibility shall be distributed. Underlying the development of the respective roles of courts and legislatures is a principle that each is to effect those reforms for which its processes make it the superior instrumentality.[20] The changes noted—increasing maturity of the legal system and increasing limitations upon the potentiality for law reform in legislatures—bear directly upon the practical application of these principles. If courts are to continue to uphold these principles and to fulfill their share of this responsibility as effectively as in the past, they must be willing in the future to overrule precedents more frequently than in the past.

STRIKING A NEW BALANCE

Concern about potential clashes between decisions and statutes—between courts and legislatures—is responsible for the reluctance of some judges to overrule precedents. But courts and legislatures need not be viewed as antagonists vying for supremacy in lawmaking. Developments in the area of tort immunities illustrate this point.

The propriety of judicial modification of precedents granting immunities has been sharply disputed; decisions have been divided on the question. [21] When precedents have been overruled, dissenting opinions have commonly argued that the responsibility for reform of immunity doctrines should have been left to the legislature.[22] Significantly, in some jurisdictions where precedents for immunity have been overruled, legislatures have promptly enacted statutes modifying the new decisional doctrines. Some critics have advanced these instances as evidence against the wisdom of judicial creativity in this area. But the net result cannot rightly be described as statutory frustration of attempted reform. No instance has been found in which the legislature restored the immunity to its former scope. Rather, a typical solution is to restore immunity above a specified amount, such as 10,000 dollars per per-

---

[20] Compare Peck, "The Role of the Courts and Legislatures in the Reform of Tort Law," 48 *Minn. L. Rev.* 265 (1963).

[21] Examples of decisions overruling precedents are cited in the Appendix. Examples of decisions adhering to precedents recognizing immunities are: McDermott v. St. Mary's Hosp. Corp., 144 Conn. 417, 133 A.2d 608 (1957); Knecht v. Saint Mary's Hosp., 392 Pa. 75, 140 A.2d 30 (1958). See also Vendrell v. School Dist. No. 26C, 360 P.2d 282 (Ore. 1961) (court cannot set aside a government immunity created by constitution).

[22] Among the overruling cases collected in the Appendix, there were such dissenting opinions in, for example, *Muskopf*, 55 Cal. 2d at 221, 359 P.2d at 463, 11 Cal. Rep. at 95; *Molitor*, 18 Ill. 2d at 29, 163 N.E.2d at 98; *Parker*, 361 Mich. at 29, 105 N.W.2d at 15; *Collopy*, 27 N.J. at 48, 61, 141 A.2d at 287, 294; *Avellone*, 165 Ohio St. at 478, 135 N.E.2d at 417.

son.[23] The combination of judicial decision and legislative reaction thus accomplishes a reform that encourages the use of liability insurance as a protection for accident victims while yet continuing the immunity as a protection against disastrously high judgments.

Courts alone would not have reached this result because the pragmatic compromise of abandoning immunity up to a specified dollar limit is foreign to accustomed judicial method. Legislatures alone could have reached this solution, but it is plain that they would not have done so as soon, if at all, had the courts declined to overrule their precedents sustaining immunity. In choosing the best among the possible rules open to them without transgressing limits of judicial function, these courts moved further toward rejecting immunities than the legislature chose to go. But in so doing they overcame legislative inertia, a potent force that otherwise would have delayed or defeated attempts at reform. These developments may be viewed as illustrating not merely the possibility of clash between decisional and statutory creativity but also the possibility of their serving in combination to bring about reform that neither alone would have been likely to achieve.

The conception that the court's role in overruling precedents is complementary to the role of the legislature in law reform can be given practical application by the court's postponing the effective date of the overruling pronouncement until the legislature has had opportunity to consider the problem.[24] More will be said on this subject in Chapter 2. Even if such a device is not used, the fact that the judicial decision is subject to statutory modification is of course implicit in the acknowledged obligation of the court to respect and enforce the statutes duly enacted. A court, then, should not refrain from correcting outmoded doctrine for fear of being chastised by the legislature's enactment of a statute restoring the old doctrine. Even in the unlikely event that a statute fully and unqualifiedly restores the overruled doctrine, its enactment should not be seen as a slap on the court's wrist or as an incident in a power struggle, but simply as a proper manifestation of the

---

[23] For example, N.J. Rev. Stat. Ann. § 2A: 53A-8 (Supp. 1967). See La Parre v. Y.M.C.A., 30 N.J. 225, 152 A.2d 340 (1959). Other illustrations of reform accomplished by the combination of judicial overruling and legislative reaction are cited in Paul J. Mishkin and Clarence Morris, *On Law In Courts* (1965), p. 316; Peck, "The Role of the Courts and Legislatures," pp. 285–293; Keeton, "Creative Continuity in the Law of Torts," 75 *Harv. L. Rev.* 463, 474 (1962). See also Brody, "Modifying Charitable Immunity," 41 *B.U.L. Rev.* 199 (1961).

[24] See Spanel v. Mounds View School Dist. No. 621, 264 Minn. 279, 292, 118 N.W.2d 795, 803 (1962).

political will through the institution designed for such expressions. As a practical matter, moreover, if there are sound reasons for the court's decision on the substantive rule in question, it is most unlikely that it will be politically possible for the legislature to undo wholly the reform accomplished by the judicial decision.

Thus, acknowledging always that the legislature can act on a matter if it will and that the range of pragmatic solutions open to a legislature is broader, the court should aim at achieving the best solution it can in the absence of a controlling statute, rather than declining to act because only the legislature can reach what the court might regard as an ideal solution.

Much as courts and legislatures need not be competitors, stability and change themselves may be viewed not as mutually repugnant but as potentially complementary values.

Consider a proposal for reforming the rules of law, still prevailing in many states, against contribution among tortfeasors. The early decisions denying contribution were based on the premise that the law should not aid wrongdoers.[25] It happens, however, that one of two persons guilty of different kinds of fault in bringing harm to a third person for which both are liable may be thought to be innocent in relation to the other, though a wrongdoer in relation to the third person. Thus, one who is only vicariously liable has been allowed indemnity from the other for whose misdeed he is legally responsible.[26] Even in relation to tortfeasors who are in pari delicto, refusal to award contribution may be attacked as inconsistent with a premise, more fundamental than refusal to aid wrongdoers, that losses should be borne by those whose wrongdoing brought them about. It is argued that one of the implications of this premise of liability based on fault, underlying most of tort law, is that none of several wrongdoers should be allowed to escape responsibility completely, especially not by a plaintiff's choice to proceed against one among potential defendants on whimsical or sinister grounds. Moreover, it is argued that distribution of the loss

[25] The rule of no contribution among tortfeasors appears to have had its origin in Merryweather v. Nixan, 8 Term R. 186, 101 Eng. Rep. 1337 (K.B. 1799), involving intentional misconduct of two persons acting in concert; the claim of one of them for contribution "rested upon what was, in the eyes of the law, entirely his own deliberate wrong." William L. Prosser, *Torts* (3rd ed. 1964), § 47, p. 273. See also Reath, "Contribution Between Persons Jointly Charged for Negligence—Merryweather v. Nixan," 12 *Harv. L. Rev.* 176 (1898).

[26] Prosser, *Torts* (3rd ed. 1964), § 47, p. 279.

20

among the several wrongdoers is a closer adherence to this fundamental premise than is refusal to allow contribution.

This is a criticism in which one of several identifiable premises of substantial segments of tort doctrine is invoked as more fundamental than that supporting a particular segment of doctrine. A court's acceptance of this kind of argument as a basis for overruling precedent,[27] or for deciding a case of first impression in its own jurisdiction contrary to the heavy weight of precedent elsewhere,[28] is a kind of creativity that involves a distinct shift in lines of doctrine, but in a way that minimizes the offense to continuity.

Contrast the foregoing argument for judicial acceptance of contribution with a modern argument for preserving the rule of no contribution —namely, that in practice the defendant from whom the plaintiff collects on his claim usually is a better loss distributor than the fellow wrongdoer from whom that defendant seeks contribution.[29] Though on the side of continuity in the sense of seeking to preserve the old rule against contribution, this argument is on the side of creativity in the sense of seeking to establish a new doctrinal explanation for that result, with potentially far-reaching consequences because of the implications of the premise that loss distribution is an objective of tort law.

This kind of creativity—discovery of new reasons for sustaining old rules that are under attack—may on its face seem less of a challenge to continuity than any form of creativity adopting a new rule that produces different results. But in fact the depth of the challenge to continuity depends not alone upon the immediate impact of the rule but also upon the significance of the premises that are discarded or adopted,

[27] Compare George's Radio, Inc., v. Capital Transit Co., 126 F.2d 219 (D.C. Cir. 1942), in which the court overruled a precedent and allowed contribution between two employers whose servants' negligence had contributed to a collision that injured a third person. In a later opinion the court extended the rule of contribution to a case in which one of the defendants was personally rather than vicariously negligent and stated the rule in very broad terms. Knell v. Feltman, 174 F.2d 662 (D.C. Cir. 1949). The latter case is also interesting because of the court's appointment of amici curiae to file briefs and participate in oral argument pursuant to the court's desire in "formulating a definite contribution rule . . . to use the utmost care and to reexamine meticulously the general subject of contribution" (at 666).

[28] Ellis v. Chicago & N.W. Ry., 167 Wis. 392, 402–410, 167 N.W. 1048, 1051–1054 (1918) (dictum), is such an opinion. See Prosser, *Torts* (3rd ed. 1964), § 47, pp. 274–275.

[29] See Fowler V. Harper and Fleming James, Jr., *Torts* (1956), vol. I, § 10.2, p. 717.

their compatibility with areas of doctrine other than that immediately involved, and their potential influence in wider areas of the law. The particular illustration just given is one in which the inconsistency of the premise of criticism with the principle that liability is based on fault, and its failure to advance an alternative consistent with prevailing community attitudes,[30] stand in the way of its acceptance.

One way in which the contrast in acceptability of narrow and broad challenges to continuity may be expressed is to say that courts on occasion depart from continuity in rule but, even when so doing, preserve continuity in principle.[31] The qualification must be added, however, that not even principles are immutable. Both their meaning and the scope of their influence are subject to change; even now the meaning and influence of the principle of liability based on fault are undergoing modification.[32] The contrast between principles and rules that is relevant at this point concerns methods of change rather than susceptibility to change. The narrow propositions commonly called rules are on occasion changed abruptly; that is, precedents are overruled. The broadest propositions, to which the term "principle" is applied, are as near to immutability as anything in law. Because of their extreme degree of generality, however, they do not severely obstruct needed reform. They are imprecise,[33] and rules or criticisms of rules cannot be derived from them merely by an exercise of logic. Indeed, a principle is not an accurate expression of the essence of many, if any, rules, because rules usually represent the product of interaction of more than one principle. Thus continuity in principle in the face of a change in

[30] With respect to an alternative very different from imposing liability on the "better loss distributor," see the discussion of the principle of distinctive risk, below, Chapter 9.

[31] See Pound, "Survey of the Conference Problems," 14 *U. Cinc. L. Rev.* 324, 328–332 (1940) (Cincinnati Conference on the Status of the Rule of Judicial Precedent), reproduced in Henry M. Hart, Jr., and Albert M. Sacks, *The Legal Process* (Tent. ed. 1958), pp. 612–616; Seavey, "The Waterworks Cases and Stare Decisis," 66 *Harv. L. Rev.* 84, 86 (1952).

[32] See below, Chapter 9.

[33] Compare *Restatement, Restitution* (1937), introductory note, p. 11: "The rules stated in the Restatement of this Subject depend for their validity upon certain basic assumptions in regard to what is required by justice in the various situations. In this Topic, these are stated in the form of principles. They cannot be stated as rules since either they are too indefinite to be of value in a specific case or, for historical or other reasons, they are not universally applied. They are distinguished from rules in that they are intended only as general guides for the conduct of the courts and are not intended to express that universality of application to particular cases which is characteristic of the statements made in subsequent chapters."

22

rule may mean no more than that no principle speaks directly to the difference between the old and the new rule, and either rule can be reconciled with accepted principles.

But there is also continuity of principle in a more basic sense—in the sense of guiding decisions both by placing outside limits on the scope of choice and by influencing the choice within that scope. To the extent that principles are effective guides, they are amenable to judicial creativity, but change in such broadly generalized propositions as these comes about through a process not aptly described as an "overruling of precedent." A principle may be modified in consequence of an extended sequence of particular decisions, but even when an inventory discloses that a change has occurred, the opinion acknowledging the change is more likely to say merely that the old principle is no longer valid than to say that it is overruled. The choice of expression in this instance is more defensible than in those instances in which courts that are plainly overruling a more specific proposition decline to say so and insist upon leaving the reader to infer what has happened—as if hoping to soften criticism, even self-criticism, by obscuring the creative character of their action.

With respect to rules, as distinguished from principles, courts have both the power to overrule and the responsibility for exercising the power. Restraint in its exercise is essential to continuity, but as already observed, abstention defeats continuity. Even beyond such yielding to creativity to serve continuity itself, demands for continuity must on occasion be sacrificed in some degree to serve greater needs of creative re-examination of court-made law. Even when acting to serve these needs, however, a court may build its creative thought upon a foundation of established concepts in whose implications are found support for departing from the precedent under re-examination. The judicial method that invokes stare decisis even in challenging a particular application of it is characteristic of opinions overruling precedents in a legal system founded on the principle that grounds of decision shall be related in some reasoned way to established concepts.[34] This form of ju-

[34] See Hart and Sacks, *The Legal Process*, pp. 588–589. As an example of an opinion invoking stare decisis explicitly while overruling precedents, see Hargrove v. Town of Cocoa Beach, 96 So. 2d 130, 134 (Fla. 1957); in overruling prior decisions that held a municipal corporation immune from liability for the torts of police officers the court said: "To support the [new] rule we hearken back to our original Florida precedent, City of Tallahassee v. Fortune [3 Fla. 19 (1850)] . . . Our judicial forebears there held that where an individual suffers a special personal damage not common to the community but proximately resulting from the

of first impression since the determinative rule comes into being only at the time of decision and is applied to a transaction that occurred at some time past. There is, of course, that ancient fallacy that the law is not retroactive because it existed all the time, though the court has just now discovered it. But lawyers and judges have a customary way of speaking about their own cases of first impression that is more candid. They say, with justifiable pride of craftsmanship, "We made new law in that case."

The retroactivity involved in deciding issues of first impression rarely provokes adverse reaction, and much lawmaking by courts occurs in this way. Indeed, in a substantial percentage of appellate litigation at least one of the advocates claims to be presenting one or more issues of first impression, emphasizing his policy arguments and the court's freedom of choice, believing his chances of success to be better by this route of distinguishing precedents than by the route of persuading the court that precedents cover the issue and require a decision in his favor.

The second of the established patterns of retroactive judicial lawmaking involves overruling. Even among those taking a relatively conservative view concerning the creative role of courts, it is commonly assumed that overruling decisions will be given retroactive application to the case at hand.[2] In the light of this assumption, the consensus that it is a proper function of the courts occasionally to overrule precedents is itself evidence that objections to retroactive creativity, though forceful as a restraining influence, are yet inconclusive.

With few exceptions, nevertheless, individual decisions overruling existing precedents provoke criticism, and broadly stated arguments against judicial lawmaking are commonly part of such criticism. Thus it happens that a recitation of traditions of prospective judicial lawmaking is part of the relevant rejoinder to arguments against retroactive as well as prospective lawmaking.

TRADITIONAL PROSPECTIVE JUDICIAL LAWMAKING

The tradition of judicial lawmaking includes ample precedents for judicial action the prospective effects of which are at least part of the justification for the action. Seven thoroughly traditional techniques of acting with prospective effect can be identified.

[2] See, for example, Shepherd v. Consumers Coop. Ass'n, 384 S.W.2d 635 (Mo. 1964).

1. Reporting judicial actions. Perhaps any system of reporting the judicial action taken in individual cases implies a conscious concern with the prospective effect of these actions as precedents rather than merely concern with such objectives as notice to the parties and regularity of the disposition of their controversy. In any event, the common law tradition has long recognized this prospective effect of decisions as precedents for guiding future decisions.

2. Reporting reasons. The common law tradition extends to reporting not merely actions taken but also reasons stated. Again, the purpose goes beyond that of informing the parties to the controversy. Reasons always are of more general application than to the case at hand and others exactly like it. Reasons, then, have even more broadly prospective effect than orders themselves.

3. Reporting alternative reasons. Often a judicial opinion states alternative reasons for the result reached. This happens when there are two or more independent ways of sustaining the result, each of which the court considers persuasive. The force of each such reason as precedent is somewhat reduced by the increased likelihood that the case will later be distinguished. That is, when the case is cited as precedent for one of two alternative points, it may be explained away on the ground that the second point was adequate to sustain the judgment and that the court may not have examined the first with full care. On the other hand, the potential prospective effect of the opinion is expanded because it advances not one but several points of precedent.

4. Reporting the persuasive rather than the narrowest possible reason. The narrowest possible ground of decision is rarely the ground persuasive to the court. If a court reports accurately why it decided as it did, the broader reasons will apply to still more cases of yet undecided types, thus further increasing the prospective quality of the court's action.

If one insisted that a court state the narrowest possible reasons rather than the actually persuasive reasons for its decision, misleading judicial pronouncements would result, defeating the very predictability of law that adherence to stare decisis is intended to serve.

Consider, for example, the case of *State Rubbish Collectors Ass'n v. Siliznoff.*[3] In a suit by the association upon notes by which Siliznoff undertook to pay $1850 for the account of a member whose business

[3] 38 Cal. 2d 330, 240 P.2d 282 (1952) (Traynor, J.).

Siliznoff's competitive activities had affected, Siliznoff "cross-complained" for cancellation of the notes and for damages for assault. The Supreme Court of California sustained a verdict and judgment for Siliznoff on both claims, despite the fact that the threats that were made, being threats of future rather than immediate physical harm, failed to meet the requirements established by precedent for assault.

Observe the wide range of choice that was open to the California court, without risk of its decision being taken as a serious challenge to continuity. It might have decided for the association on the ground that though there were no previous California cases directly in point, it was plain that Siliznoff was seeking damages under circumstances in which most courts theretofore would have denied recovery—no assault, no cause of action for intentionally inflicted emotional suffering, no recovery. Or the court might have decided for Siliznoff on the narrowly creative ground of overruling precedents defining assault and redefining it to include cases concerned with threats of physical harm in the near future. Instead, Justice Roger Traynor adopted a more broadly creative theory. He reviewed the whole development of remedies in tort for mental suffering and recognized liability in the instant case on a theory outside the category of assault.

This last course is in truth as clearly a departure from precedent as the second course would have been. But it is less patently so because it challenges only a negative more often implied than expressed—namely, that when decisional law has purported to deal with the problem rather than leaving it wholly unconsidered, one cannot recover by setting up a new theory rather than bringing his case within a recognized category of liability. There can be no doubt that earlier decisions defining assault in terms of threats of immediate harm were generally understood as precedents for denying recovery completely and not merely for rejecting the theory of assault. This aspect of the precedents is abrogated by *Siliznoff*.

It might be argued that beyond its effect on doctrines of tort law *Siliznoff* tends more to abrogate—or to confirm an accomplished abrogation—than to support a significant facet of the doctrine of stare decisis as once understood. At some point in the development of the common law, it came to be a rather generally shared assumption that there were no causes of action other than those already recognized in precedents. That assumption was not so generally shared in the early history of the common law. Nor is it, nor should it be, today. Rather than assuming that there are no causes of action except those recognized in precedents, or conversely that there is a cause of action unless denied by precedent, it seems wiser and more equitable to start the inquiry neutrally when there is no precedent in point. Whatever one derives from *Siliznoff* on this point is largely speculative, however, since the decisional law that preceded it, rather than offering no precedent on threats of harm in the near but not immediate future, had been denying recovery in such cases. The difficulty of finding cases that explicitly declared this to be so arises from the very fact that the point was so well understood that it was rarely thought worth expressing.

Siliznoff is inconsistent with the principle sometimes urged that a court in acting creatively should adopt the narrowest possible ground of departure that will cover the case at hand. In fact, though that practice is urged in the name of continuity, it is less conducive to predictability of decisions than is the practice of expressing the broader grounds that actually guide the court to its decision. This remains true even though expressing grounds broader than necessary for decision may befuddle efforts to find a clear line of demarcation between holding and dictum. A court may appropriately choose to express a narrower ground of decision when its attraction to the broader principle falls short of conviction.[4] But when conviction has been reached, an opinion placing the decision on a narrower ground is misleading. In contrast, the *Siliznoff* opinion, with its broad explanation of the result reached, gives warning that this area of law is in course of change.

5. *Reporting concurring opinions.* Though the judges of appellate courts do not feel obligated to explain their judicial votes in full by disclosing in every case the extent to which they agree or disagree with each thought expressed in the court's opinion, it is nevertheless common practice to express differences of opinion on some occasions through concurring opinions. Such concurring opinions often serve as the robins that foretell a new spring. They give notice of the possibility of change by expressing minority views that may become majority views in the future for a variety of reasons—among them, changing views and changing personnel of the court. Coincidentally, they reduce the force of the majority opinion as precedent, increasing the likelihood that the rule there stated will be abandoned at some time in the future. A striking and rather unusual example is a concurring opinion published in 1961, suggesting that re-examination of the doctrine of as-

[4] Compare Llewellyn, *The Common Law Tradition*, pp. 388–389, 427–429.

sumption of risk would be in order when the court was next presented with a case in which views concerning assumption of risk might be crucial.[5] The re-examination soon occurred.[6]

6. *Reporting dissenting opinions.* The common practice of reporting dissenting opinions is another traditional technique of prospective judicial lawmaking, since such opinions prepare the way for change in a way closely comparable to that of concurring opinions.

7. *Including obiter dicta in opinions.* It is sometimes argued that broad statements of reasons for decision, such as those relied upon in *Siliznoff*, are obiter dicta rather than holdings. Even if one insists upon such a definition of the distinction between holding and dictum, however, the prospectively creative character of these broad pronouncements remains.[7]

They give notice of the way in which the court is likely to resolve the issue with which they deal when it is squarely presented, and they tend to be self-fulfilling prophecies, even if not binding as precedents, because they have some weight as considered expressions. Moreover, whether or not so intended, obiter dicta, insofar as they express views not fully developed in existing precedents, are primarily prospective in influence. Indeed, it is more likely than not in routine situations that they will be exclusively prospective in application. It is true that such a dictum might have retroactive application to previous transactions brought into issue thereafter, but it is more likely that even the first judicial application of the dictum will concern a transaction occurring after the dictum was published. The common practice of including dicta of this type in opinions suggests a consensus that this is permissible judicial behavior—a consensus that undermines the notion that the prospective effect of judicial opinions is supposed to be wholly incidental to retroactive decisional application.

The seven techniques of prospective judicial lawmaking thus far considered are thoroughly traditional. Each of the first four illustrates prospective lawmaking that might be regarded as presumptively con-

[5] Baird v. Cornelius, 12 Wis. 2d 284, 303, 107 N.W.2d 278, 288 (1961).

[6] McConville v. State Farm Mut. Auto. Ins. Co., 15 Wis. 2d 374, 113 N.W.2d 14 (1962).

[7] For another illustration of this point, consider Duffy v. Bill, 32 N.J. 278, 160 A.2d 822 (1960), in which a railroad company's legal duty with respect to hazards at a grade crossing is declared to be expanded. It might be argued that this declaration is dictum, because the court proceeds to hold as a matter of law that the company's failure in this instance to provide extra precautions was not a violation of the stated duty. Whatever this declaration may be called, the fact remains that it can be expected to have very significant prospective effect.

summated, even as to future cases somewhat different from that before the court, though it remains to be seen whether, when confronted with a case arguably within the scope of the earlier action, the court will find a way to distinguish it. The fifth, sixth, and seventh techniques illustrate preparatory steps in a process of lawmaking to be consummated in later judicial action. Consider, now, some additional illustrations of preparatory steps that may be regarded as less traditional, though instances of their use can be found.

Declaring that dicta are included to give notice. As already observed, dicta have long served a function of notice about the way the court is likely to respond to an issue when it is squarely presented. Ordinarily the function of giving notice has not been a declared objective, but occasionally an explicit statement of this intention appears in a judicial opinion. Such a statement increases the force of the prospective pronouncement by declaring it to be purposive and legitimate rather than merely a coincidental by-product of the court's legitimate work.

An example appears in an opinion of the Wisconsin Supreme Court concerning a claim for prenatal injury. The court determined that the evidence presented was insufficient to support a finding that the defendant's conduct caused a prenatal injury. This was, of course, all that was required for disposition of the case at hand. "However," the court added, "the importance of this problem compels us to point out the present status of the law." Having thus explained why they were doing so, the court reviewed the shift of the weight of precedents from various states concerning prenatal injuries and observed the dubious reliability of the Wisconsin precedent.[8]

Declaring that a stated question of law is undecided, or that decision is reserved. It often happens that it is quite generally understood that the law of a state on some identifiable issue is settled by indications of an assumption underlying many opinions. For example, when the *Siliznoff* case arose in California, no doubt it was generally considered to be the settled law that one could not recover damages for mental suffering caused by a threat of future impact, as distinguished from a threat of an impact sufficiently immediate to constitute an assault. Yet this understanding did not depend on an explicit decision that no theory of recovery other than assault was available. Perhaps, as already suggested, the reason for absence of such explicit holdings was the fact that the understanding was so clear and unchallenged. The *Siliznoff*

---

[8] Puhl v. Milwaukee Auto. Ins. Co., 8 Wis. 2d 343, 354–357, 99 N.W.2d. 163, 169–171 (1960).

opinion, then, had the effect of overruling that understood rule, though the court did not find it necessary to say they were overruling any identified precedent.

In the context of such a general understanding on some issue not actually before the court for decision, another way in which a court may act prospectively is to say in its opinion that it regards the stated issue as unsettled or that it will be treated as an issue of first impression when it is next squarely presented to the court. This can be an important step in the process of making law on that issue.

In an opinion delivered in 1966, the Minnesota court treated the issues of parental and interspousal immunities in a way that might be regarded as illustrating this technique. The court felt obliged to deal more directly with another issue: the immunity of a child against a claim of his parent caused by the child's negligent driving. They explicitly declared that they were "overruling" the bar's expectation that the court would recognize such an immunity. With respect to a parent's immunity against suit by a child and one spouse's immunity against suit by the other, the court was more cautious. "An adjudication involving a review of the immunity doctrine in these situations must await a full presentation in an adversary setting between litigants to whom the issue is one of genuine moment and concern, and thus justiciable." [9]

Declaring that those joining in an opinion will consider an identified precedent as not binding for future cases. Members of a court who are pressed to overrule an outmoded precedent may nevertheless decline to do so, acting in deference to interests affected by reliance upon the precedent—for example, the interests of a church whose governing board declined to buy liability insurance because they relied upon a precedent for immunity. In this setting, an opinion of the court, or a concurring or dissenting opinion, may declare that those joining in the opinion adhere to the precedent for the case at hand, and other cases based on transactions occurring before this opinion is filed, but give notice that as to claims arising thereafter they will consider themselves free to re-examine the substantive issue on the merits as if it were an issue of first impression—free of the restraints incident to reliance on the precedents. [10]

Declaring that a determination on an issue of first impression shall

<hr/>

[9] Balts v. Balts, 273 Minn. 419, 142 N.W.2d 66 (1966).

[10] See the concurring opinion of Greenhill, J., in Watkins v. Southcrest Baptist Church, 399 S.W.2d 530, 535 (Tex. 1966).

apply only to future cases. On rare occasions courts have, in deciding issues of first impression, confined the effect of their rulings to future cases. For example, when the Supreme Court of Ohio ruled legislative divorces invalid, it declared that its decision would affect only future divorces.[11]

PROSPECTIVE OVERRULING

In light of the long tradition of prospective judicial lawmaking by various means, it is hardly bold to assert that overruling a precedent prospectively is legitimate. Yet, it has been argued, first, that courts should refrain from overruling prospectively because declarations of new rules would be only obiter dicta if not applied retroactively and, second, that a prospective overruling would be merely an advisory opinion and therefore, in some jurisdictions at least, beyond the scope of constitutional judicial power. The fallacy of both arguments has been effectively exposed.[12] They fail to take due account of the fact that the new rule could have been dispositive of the litigation and was fully considered by the court. That a court might have reached the same result by a different line of reasoning does not deprive the judicial opinion of its quality as the court's own explanation of its considered choice concerning the potentially dispositive rule.

Consider, for example, a case in which a defense of charitable immunity is supported by precedent. Among the grounds upon which a court might decide for the defendant are these: first, that the rule of immunity is sound on the merits and is reaffirmed; second, that the rule of immunity is undesirable, but changing it is a task for the legislature, not the court; third, that the rule of immunity is undesirable and is overruled, but in deference to the interests of those who have in some way acted in reliance on the immunity the overruling is held inapplicable to claims arising before the court's opinion is filed. Few, if any, persons would question that a decision on the first or the second of these grounds should be recognized as a holding, fully entitled to the respect accorded to precedents. If the court decides for the defendant not on one of these two grounds but on the third, consistency requires that this, too, be recognized as a holding. Conversely, if a court's decla-

[11] Bingham v. Miller, 17 Ohio 445 (1848). My attention was directed to this illustration by Schaefer, "The Control of 'Sunbursts': Techniques of Prospective Overruling," 22 *Record of N.Y.C. Bar Ass'n* 394, 395 (1967).

[12] See, for example, Currier, "Time and Change in Judge-Made Law: Prospective Overruling," 51 *Va. L. Rev.* 201, 216–220 (1965).

ration that it adheres to an old rule merely because it chooses not to overrule retroactively is mere dictum, then so too is a court's declaration that it adheres to an old rule on its merits or because it thinks the problem one for the legislature; in each case it can be said that either of the other two of these three lines of reasoning would have produced the same judgment. If that prevents a stated reason for decision from being a holding, little indeed of what courts say could ever be classified as holdings.

Whatever one's definition of holding may be, courts customarily include obiter dicta in their opinions, and their doing so is often extremely useful. Thus let the pronouncement be treated as dictum if one wishes to call it that. It is then a dictum especially useful in predicting future decisions, since it almost certainly will be transformed into a holding when the question next comes before the court. In short, if we look to fact and function rather than to form, prospective overruling by courts is not the exercise of a basically new power, but only a relatively less familiar way of exercising a familiar power.

Prospective overruling has been urged by distinguished commentators. John Henry Wigmore and Benjamin Cardozo were among its early advocates,[13] and Cardozo gave impetus to the novel judicial method in his *Sunburst* opinion,[14] sustaining its use by a state supreme court in the face of an attack on constitutional grounds. The early comments favoring prospective overruling, though not excluding its use in tort cases, adverted primarily to its advantages for cases in which some change of position in reliance upon established precedent is ordinarily more easily demonstrated—cases within the areas of criminal, contract, and property law. But, in addition to instances of prospective overruling outside the area of torts,[15] there has been a burst of such activity in tort cases.

[13] See Schaefer, "The Control of 'Sunbursts'"; Levy, "Realist Jurisprudence and Prospective Overruling," 109 *U. Pa. L. Rev.* 1, 7–25 (1960). See also Comment, "Prospective Overruling and Retroactive Application in the Federal Courts," 71 *Yale L. J.* 907 (1962); Annot., 85 A.L.R. 262 (1933). The earliest cited example of prospective overruling is Jones v. Woodstock Iron Co., 95 Ala. 551, 10 So. 635 (1892). As we have seen in note 11 above, however, Justice Schaefer (p. 395) calls attention to an even earlier instance of nonretroactive judicial decision that did not involve overruling a precedent.

[14] Great Northern Ry. v. Sunburst Oil & Ref. Co., 287 U.S. 358 (1932).

[15] Concerning the use of this technique particularly in constitutional litigation, see Mishkin, "The Supreme Court, 1964 Term—Foreword: The High Court, the Great Writ, and the Due Process of Time and Law," 79 *Harv. L. Rev.* 56 (1965). See also Currier, "Time and Change in Judge-Made Law"; Bender, "The Retroactive Effect of an Overruling Constitutional Decision: Mapp v. Ohio," 110 *U. Pa.*

This increased activity commenced with a series of immunity cases reaching state courts of last resort in 1959–61. Within a period of fourteen months, and in the order named, the supreme courts of Illinois, Michigan, and Wisconsin [16] prospectively overruled precedents on this subject. This technique was used as a way around the argument that a retroactive ruling would have been unfair to institutions whose governing boards had, in reliance upon immunity, failed to provide for such claims by liability insurance or otherwise. The New Jersey court, faced with the same argument just before this series of decisions, considered prospective overruling but chose instead to overrule retroactively because it was satisfied that there had been no justifiable reliance on the unimpaired continuance of the immunity invoked in that case.[17]

Each of the three 1959–61 decisions that overruled prospectively nevertheless applied the new rule retroactively to the claim before the court.[18] The opinions in two of the cases justified this action, in part, as being designed to encourage socially beneficial attacks upon outmoded doctrine.[19]

One's views on this special twist of doctrine might be colored by his reaction to rewarding peaceful protest more than fidelity to declared law. Apart from that diversionary perspective, this selective retroactive application produces distinctions perhaps more difficult to justify than either wholly prospective or wholly retroactive overruling. It might seem fair to use public funds to reward this benefaction of legal doctrine, particularly since the reward amounts only to compensation for accidental harm the benefactor has suffered. Except by the grace of a

---

L. Rev. 650 (1962); Comment, "Prospective Overruling and Retroactive Application in the Federal Courts," 71 *Yale L. J.* 907 (1962); Annot., 14 L. Ed. 2d 992 (1966).

[16] Molitor v. Kaneland Community Unit Dist. No. 302, 18 Ill. 2d 11, 26–29, 163 N.E.2d 89, 96–98 (1959); *cert. denied*, 362 U.S. 968 (1960). Parker v. Port Huron Hosp., 361 Mich. 1, 26–28, 105 N.W.2d 1, 13–15 (1960). Kojis v. Doctors Hosp., 12 Wis. 2d 367, 107 N.W.2d 131, *modified on rehearing*, 107 N.W.2d 292 (1961).

[17] Dalton v. St. Luke's Catholic Church, 27 N.J. 22, 25–26, 141 A.2d 273, 274–275 (1958).

[18] Concerning extension to other closely connected cases, see Molitor v. Kaneland Community Unit Dist. No. 302, 24 Ill. 2d 467, 182 N.E.2d 145 (1962).

[19] Molitor v. Kaneland Community Unit Dist. No. 302, 18 Ill. 2d 11, 28, 163 N.E.2d 89, 97 (1959); Kojis v. Doctors Hosp., 12 Wis. 2d 367, 374, 107 N.W.2d 131, 292, 294. A second reason stated in each of these opinions is that if the new rule were announced without application to the instant case, "such announcement would amount to mere dictum." This point seems to be associated with the untenable view, discussed earlier in this chapter, that prospective effect of court action is supposed to be, in form at least, wholly incidental to retroactive effect.

legislature,[20] however, public funds are not used to pay the reward under this rule. Rather, the unfortunate institution that happens to have the test case brought against it bears the cost, while institutions similarly situated escape cost. Moreover, the reward is bestowed on the plaintiff for being first in time in the appellate court—first, that is, after the ripening of a potential readiness of the court to overrule the precedent in question.

This combination of partly prospective and partly retroactive overruling offers only a little more encouragement to attacks on outmoded doctrine than the inducement a claimant and his attorney would find in the hope of persuading the court to overrule retroactively. The advantage from this added degree of encouragement, such as it may be, probably is outweighed by the disadvantage of uneven treatment of claimants and formerly immune institutions. It is true that some unevenness is an inevitable consequence of any change in doctrine, regardless of the choice among methods of change. But it seems preferable that a court reduce the element of unevenness more than is possible under decisions applying a new rule retroactively only to the case before the court, or to that and closely related cases.

TECHNIQUES OF PROSPECTIVE OVERRULING

That blend of retroactive and prospective overruling in which the new rule is applied retroactively only to the case at hand illustrates the point that more than one technique of partly prospective overruling can be devised. In fact, a congeries of possibilities exists, representing differing blends of retroactive and prospective effect to the court's newly fashioned rule. One may also see these as various ways of limiting the scope of application of the decision. From this perspective a determination that the new rule shall apply only to specified classes of future transactions is a prospective limitation—that is, a limitation of the new rule to prospective application—rather than a prospective overruling.[21]

Definitions of the future transactions to which a new rule applies may vary in detail. For example, it may be determined that the new

20 Public funds were in fact used in the sequel to *Molitor;* the Illinois legislature appropriated $750,000 to relieve the defendant school district from the crushing burden of judgments in excess of insurance limits in favor of several of the children to whose claims the "reward" for attacking the outmoded immunity was extended. See Larson v. Kaneland Community Unit Dist. No. 302, 52 Ill. App. 2d 209, 201 N.E.2d 865 (2d Dist. 1964).

21 See Mishkin, "The Supreme Court, 1964 Term—Foreword," p. 58.

rule will apply to all cases based on incidents occurring after the opinion is filed; or, in order to provide reasonable notice to parties whose interests might be affected or to provide reasonable opportunity for the state's legislature to consider the issue, the new rule may be applied only to cases based on incidents occurring after a specified interval.

Definitions of past transactions to which a new rule applies may also vary in detail. As already noted, some courts have chosen to apply a new rule only to the case at hand or to that case and a very limited number of others closely associated with it. Another body of cases has defined past transactions affected by the new rule in a way distinctively associated with liability insurance.

For a long time, a minority view has rejected charitable immunity to the extent that the institution was protected by liability insurance, though continuing to recognize the immunity otherwise.[22] A somewhat different and more defensible use of the fact of liability insurance occurs when a court limits the scope of its retroactive overruling of an immunity to the amount of liability insurance applying to the claim, declining to extend its ruling to uninsured amounts on the ground that the governing boards of charitable institutions may justifiably rely on immunity from damages beyond their insurance coverage.[23] The extent to which a charity's governing board actually relies on immunity when purchasing low-limits liability insurance may be debatable. This method has some appeal, however, as a less drastic measure than full-scale retroactive overruling. It uses liability insurance as a shock absorber; the rates insurance companies charged their policyholders may have been too low because of reliance on the precedent, but it is possible to allow appropriate recoupment of losses in higher rates for later periods.[24] The blow is thus cushioned; many policyholders will pay a little extra but none very much. This blend of prospective and retroactive application can be seen as a way of pushing toward the rule that is preferred on the merits as far as possible while yet avoiding severe impact on those having reliance interests.

These illustrations are sufficient to demonstrate that the methods of overruling are numerous and diverse. One who puts together the vari-

[22] For example, O'Connor v. Boulder Colorado Sanitarium Ass'n, 105 Colo. 259, 96 P.2d 835 (1939), 133 A.L.R. 819 (1941); Annot., 25 A.L.R.2d 29, 89, 139–142 (1952).

[23] Myers v. Drozda, 180 Neb. 183, 141 N.W.2d 852 (1966).

[24] Concerning the reliance interests of liability insurance companies and the recoupment of losses caused by changes in law, see below, pp. 42–43.

ous blends of retroactive and prospective application suggested even by this brief discussion discovers many possible combinations. The judicial and other writings on this subject have as yet proceeded only a little way toward exposition of the standards for choosing among the many available blends.

Prospective overruling, then, is a new and relatively undeveloped judicial technique in a sense. But various methods of prospective judicial lawmaking are within our legal tradition. Prospective overruling of decisional law is not a departure from the traditional function of courts, but a new way of discharging a function courts have been performing since the dawn of the common-law tradition. There will be occasions, of course, when prospective lawmaking by courts is less appropriate than either retroactive lawmaking or staunch adherence to precedent. But total rejection of prospective overruling would be a crippling limitation of judicial method.

Chapter 3
Occasions for Prospective or
Retroactive Overruling

*T*HOUGH there has long been a consensus favoring occasional judicial overruling of precedents, seldom either in judicial opinions or in other writings has any attempt been made to formulate reasonably precise guidelines for determining when this power should be exercised. Still less often has attention been given to guidelines for the choice among adhering to precedent and overruling retroactively, prospectively, or with some blend of retroactive and prospective application.

Perhaps it is easier to identify than to explain how to identify appropriate occasions and appropriate methods for overruling. Moreover, the advantages of the common law method over the statutory method of developing law are relevant here: codifying guidelines on this subject would undoubtedly produce mistakes that could be avoided by feeling one's way along case by case.

It would be entirely consistent with the pursuit of this case-by-case method of developing guidelines, however, for courts to be more candid and articulate about it. At present one who seeks the sense of precedents on this question must do much reading between the lines. All too often, discussion has been almost exclusively limited to gross assertions either that lawmaking is for legislatures or that outmoded court-made rules ought to be corrected by courts. What is needed is, first, acknowledgment of the necessity of distinguishing the appropriate from the inappropriate occasions for overruling precedents, and, second, an attempt to develop a body of case law that gives courts improved guidance.

One step in the right direction is the attempt to articulate reasons for overruling in a particular case, or for not doing so, that are also reasons of general validity. Such a question of legal process, like questions of substantive law, should be open to reasoned debate.

Most formulations thus far attempted in this area have been extremely general in character, offering very little specific guidance. This state of affairs is not peculiar to American jurisdictions; the guideline that the House of Lords suggested in announcing their about-face on the question of overruling their own precedents is singularly interesting from this point of view. Their Lordships "propose, therefore, to modify their present practice and, while treating former decisions of this House as normally binding, to depart from a previous decision when it appears right to do so." [1]

Their succinct four-paragraph announcement of this important change of practice, though not explicitly so formulated, can be read as stating factors they will consider in deciding whether it is right to overrule in a particular case. Some are factors against overruling. First, precedent is an indispensable foundation for deciding individual cases. Second, adherence to precedent is the basis for orderly development of legal rules. Third, adhering to precedent provides a degree of certainty upon which people can rely in conducting their affairs. The announcement refers to two points that might be regarded as corollaries of this third factor. One is that it is undesirable to disturb retroactively the basis on which contracts, settlements, and fiscal arrangements have been made. The other is that there is especial need for certainty in criminal law. Factors the House of Lords referred to that tend to support overruling are, first, that too rigid adherence to precedent produces injustice in individual cases and, second, that it restricts proper development of the law.

In an address delivered and published shortly before the decade of distinctively accelerated overruling commenced in 1958, Justice Walter V. Schaefer of the Supreme Court of Illinois suggested that the question whether a court should overrule in a particular case "depends on whether the policies which underlie the proposed rule are strong enough to outweigh both the policies which support the existing rule and the disadvantages of making a change." [2] Though there is more than ample scope within each of the three facets of this test, at least it suggests a useful approach to the problem, around which others can join with Justice Schafer in developing more explicit guidance.

The disadvantages of change referred to are principally the distinctive disadvantages of decisional in comparison with statutory change, and they depend upon many factors. Among these are (1) the court's confidence in its understanding of the type of problem exemplified by the single case at hand in comparison with the understanding that might be attained by a legislature through investigation; (2) the de-

---

[1] [1966] 1 Weekly L.R. 1234.
[2] Walter V. Schaefer, *Precedent and Policy* (1956), p. 9.

gree of conviction about the merits of the precedent and the rule proposed in its stead, and the consistency of that appraisal with settled views of significant groups in society; (3) the scope of application and complexity of the precedent under challenge, and the feasibility of reforming it through judicial decisions on a case-by-case basis rather than through comprehensive legislation; (4) the magnitude of the change (viewed not only in terms of its impact upon particular decisions, but also in terms of its consistency with major currents of doctrine and its potential impact upon future doctrinal developments); and (5) the extent of reliance upon the precedent and, in view of such reliance, the probable extent of harm from overruling it.[3]

Reliance interests tend to support adherence to precedent and, if not strong enough to overcome factors favoring overruling, tend to favor prospective over retroactive overruling.[4] Before the various techniques of prospective overruling came to the fore—when the court's choice appeared to be one between overruling retroactively and adhering to precedent—reliance interests were an even stronger influence than now for adherence to precedent. With the added possibilities of various blends of prospective and retroactive overruling at hand, there will doubtless be a tendency to use some intermediate technique in lieu of either of the extremes.

Recognizing prospective overruling as an appropriate form of judicial action disfavors creativity in one respect: by discouraging needed retroactive changes. It favors creativity in another: by tempering the restraining influence of concern with reliance upon precedent. Thus the development of intermediate techniques may be alarming both to advocates of more active judicial creativity, who fear discouragement of retroactive overruling, and to advocates of less judicial creativity, who fear encouragement of judicial license. It is possible to guard against these potential evils without entirely foregoing the use of prospective overruling, however, and various blends of action that include prospective overruling in some degree seem desirable additions to the range of choice open to courts, especially if they are used sparingly as measures to counter the brake upon reform that results from regard for expectations arising from reliance upon precedent.

[3] See Schaefer, *Precedent and Policy*, pp. 9–13.

[4] For a very suggestive analysis of the significance of reliance interests, see Mishkin and Morris, *On Law in Courts*, pp. 295–317. See also Schaefer, "The Control of 'Sunbursts,'" pp. 407–411; Mishkin, "The Supreme Court, 1964 Term —Foreword," pp. 66–72.

The reliance interest most commonly urged in personal injury cases relates to a choice made by an alleged tortfeasor before the incident on which the tort claim is based: a choice not to obtain liability insurance. It is peculiarly appropriate that this reliance interest, depending as it does upon appraising and managing risks, be viewed in the light of whatever indications there may have been of instability of the precedent in question. Often it happens that before the actual overturning of the precedent, arguments for such action have been expressed in concurring or dissenting opinions. These can serve as notice of the unreliability of the existing precedent. Alert governing boards of the institutions enjoying immunity may provide against catastrophe by appropriate liability insurance arrangements. Thus when the precedent is finally overruled, the court has a very practical answer to the argument of reliance as a reason for declining to overrule retroactively. Moreover, the break is less abrupt than it would be in the absence of advance warnings.

It is sometimes suggested that retroactive overruling in tort cases is unfair not only to uninsured institutions, but also to liability insurers, whose rates have been set in reliance on precedent, and to the group of policyholders who will pay higher than compensatory premiums in order to make up for the losses the insurers suffer by collecting inadequate premiums over the period to which the overruling decision retroactively applies.

Some clear implications of this view demonstrate its unacceptability. First, its general acceptance would in effect disable courts from creative decisions in accident law. Second, the need for protecting the reliance interest is much less significant in this context than in the context of uninsured institutions, since the impact upon any particular insurer or insured is so much less serious. Some guarantee of this appraisal appears in the fact that ordinarily it is impossible to trace the impact of particular legal doctrines upon liability insurance rates.[5] Even when the doctrinal change is one that might promptly affect rates, as in the case of overruling an immunity,[6] there remains a contrast between the

[5] See Morris, "Enterprise Liability and the Actuarial Process—The Insignificance of Foresight," 70 *Yale L. J.* 554, 579–581 (1961).

[6] In Vendrell v. School District No. 26C, Malheur County, 226 Or. 263, 360 P.2d 282 (1961), the court construed a statute as waiving the immunity of school districts to the extent its activities are in fact covered by liability insurance purchased under the statutory authorization. 2 For the Defense 67 (Nov. 1961) reported that as a result of this decision there was an approved increase of 100 percent to 700 percent in bodily injury liability insurance premium rates for Oregon schools.

reliance of an insurer (in setting rates) and the reliance of other institutions (in choosing not to obtain insurance). A single heavy judgment against an uninsured hospital would be more likely to spell catastrophe than the number of such judgments that would fall on a single insurer. Moreover, there is a good prospect of the insurer's spreading the loss among a group that comes fairly close to corresponding with the group of policyholders who might appropriately have been required to pay higher premiums if the overruling decision had been forecast.

Beyond all this, any possible argument based on the reliance of insurers appears weaker yet when concurring or dissenting opinions, or comments in majority opinions, have given notice of the unreliability of the precedent at issue. In this respect, as in others, the candid expression of the considered view of a minority of the court that a precedent should be overruled, or the considered view of either a minority or a majority that the time for careful review of the precedent is near at hand, minimizes the offense to continuity.

General guidelines such as those presented above are hardly more than a statement of principles. Rules of application remain to be developed as the House of Lords and American courts apply these principles to particular cases. In the United States there is already a substantial and rapidly growing body of illustrative cases—as we have seen, more than ninety overruling private law decisions have been rendered within a decade. They provide both a collection of actual holdings and a library of suggestive ideas advanced in the majority and dissenting opinions.

Despite the generality of most statements about when it is appropriate for a court to overrule, there is a considerable area of agreement on the division between courts and legislatures of responsibility for reform, and even considerable agreement concerning particular applications.

It is easiest, perhaps, to find consensus on some things courts should not do. For example, they should not undertake to substitute a workmen's compensation type of system for the current law of automobile cases, although such a change is plainly within the sphere of competence of a legislature (except insofar as constitutional inhibitions may affect some aspects of a specific proposal). It is more difficult to explain *why* they should not take such action. To what extent, if at all, does this limitation depend on the major and pervasive character of the change? Or on its controversial nature? Or on the characterization of the change as political in some sense? Or on the fact that such compensation systems use schedules of benefits and pecuniary limits of liability that seem arbitrary by customary modes of judicial reasoning, though quite reasonable as expressions of political compromise?

Recent developments suggest an emerging consensus that changing the basic principle of liability from negligence to strict liability in the products liability area is not beyond judicial competence. If courts can make the change for that area, is it not also within their competence to do so for automobile cases?

In making the change in the products liability area, courts have not adopted—as yet—the suggestion advanced at various times by commentators that the measure of damages be reduced to something short of that ordinarily applied in negligence cases—for example, by disallowing compensation for pain and suffering. A major barrier to judicial adoption of a principle of strict liability for automobile cases may be an uneasiness, at the least, about whether it is appropriate for a court to scale down damages while broadening liability—because this has the ring of political compromise. This concern is perhaps coupled with a realization that, unless the measure of damages is modified, changing to strict liability is certain to produce sharp increases in automobile liability insurance rates, the high level of which is one of the major reasons the public is critical of automobile law and insurance arrangements as they stand today.

Because of the aura of political compromise involved in scaling down damages as distinguished from totally excluding specified elements from the measure of damages, perhaps it would be easier for a court to deny pain and suffering damages altogether than to institute limits besides the very permissive ones generally employed in supervising jury verdicts in negligence cases. At first blush such elimination of pain and suffering as an element of damages might also seem foreign to judicial method. But developments arguably analogous may be found.

It is often urged that various activities in society should be made to pay their own way, so persons who receive the benefits also bear the burdens and, as nearly as possible, each in proportion to his benefits. This argument is closely related to theories of unjust enrichment, which have led courts in other contexts to recognize legal rights for recoveries measured in objective terms only. The classic illustration is the right of one to get back money he paid to another under mutual mistake, as when both parties mistakenly thought the payee was the intended beneficiary of a gift the payor was commissioned to deliver for a donor. The one who received the money by mistake may suffer agony at the thought of giving up all the things he had expected to buy with it, but compensation for that is not within the theory of action. Might courts reasonably develop a theory of strict liability for economic losses caused by an activity, without tacking on damages for pain and suffering as well? If it seems so, perhaps the area of consensus at the negative end of the spectrum—concerning what courts should *not* do—will dwindle somewhat rather than increasing in the future.

Defining an area of agreement is even more difficult at the affirmative end of the spectrum than at the negative end. That is, it is harder to achieve consensus about occasions when it is clearly proper for a court to overrule. Some courts continue to declare that change is exclusively the province of the legislature even in the area of subjects producing the greatest number of overruling decisions. But at least we can identify types of problems concerning which a substantial number of jurisdictions have had overruling decisions. The topics leading in number of overruling jurisdictions during the decade commencing in 1958 are government immunities, charitable immunities, intrafamily immunities, prenatal injury, privity, and strict products liability.[7]

All but the last of these might be regarded as areas of change designed to rid the law of some rough edges—harsh deviations from ordinary standards of liability that denied certain special categories of victims any recovery for their injuries resulting from the negligent conduct of others. The last area—strict products liability—stands against any notion that judicial abrogation of precedents should be limited to sanding off rough edges of the law. It is nevertheless the case that one factor among others relevant to the propriety of overruling is the scope of the proposed change. The more pervasive the scope, the harder it is to persuade courts the change is one they can properly make. Perhaps it is more than coincidence that some of the decisions plainly abrogating precedents on products liability failed to state explicitly that they were overruling. Perhaps it is sound to say, too, that although a number of courts have abrogated their precedents on products liability, candid judicial overruling in this area is nonetheless more controversial than in the other five areas just listed.

More controversial still is the proposal that the courts should act to improve the rules of law applying when the negligence of two or more

[7] See the Appendix.

persons contributes to an injury. The stronger opposition may seem surprising from one point of view, since changes in this area might be regarded as merely dealing with rough edges wholly within the law of negligence—changes less drastic than a shift from negligence theory to strict liability, such as has occurred in the area of products liability. In another respect, however, they are changes of broad scope—affecting many more cases. Because they are highly controversial, proposals for change in this area will serve well as a subject for closer examination.

The common law, as noted in Chapter 1, developed a rule against contribution among wrongdoers. No doubt an overwhelming majority of judges today consider this a bad rule on the merits. It often imposes a loss wholly on one of two or more equally guilty wrongdoers, and on a basis that is fortuitous or worse. Similarly, the common law developed a rule of contributory negligence that leaves one of two equally guilty parties to bear an entire loss. This, too, is generally disapproved today on the merits,[8] though perhaps not so overwhelmingly as the rule against contribution. Yet only one court, an intermediate court of Illinois, has chosen to overturn the contributory negligence rule—and that decision was later reversed by a majority of the Supreme Court of that state.[9]

It is sometimes suggested that the controversial questions confronted in these two areas of doctrine cannot be answered by simply declaring a new rule in one judicial opinion—that, since a comprehensive plan of apportionment is needed, these are inappropriate areas for creative judicial action. It may be observed, however, that doctrines of apportioning damages have in fact been adopted in some instances by judicial action rather than by statute. For example, admiralty rules of apportionment are generally of decisional origin.[10] Also, a rule of compara-

[8] The reasons for disapproval of the contributory fault rule have been exhaustively developed. See, for example, Harper and James, *Torts* (1956), §§ 22.1–22.3, vol. II, pp. 1193–1209, § 22.11, vol. II, pp. 1236–1241; Prosser, *Torts* (3rd ed. 1964), § 66, pp. 443–444; Glanville L. Williams, *Joint Torts and Contributory Negligence* (1951), pt. 2; Gregory, "Loss Distribution by Comparative Negligence," 21 *Minn. L. Rev.* 1 (1936); Maloney, "From Contributory to Comparative Negligence: A Needed Law Reform," 11 *U. Fla. L. Rev.* 135 (1958); Mole and Wilson, "A Study of Comparative Negligence (pts. 1 & 2)," 17 *Cornell L. Q.* 333, 604 (1932); Peck, "Comparative Negligence and Automobile Liability Insurance," 58 *Mich. L. Rev.* 689 (1960); Philbrick, "Loss Apportionment in Negligence Cases (pts. 1 & 2)," 99 *U. Pa. L. Rev.* 572, 766 (1951); Turk, "Comparative Negligence on the March (pts. 1 & 2)," 28 *Chi.-Kent L. Rev.* 189, 304 (1950).

[9] Maki v. Frelk, 229 N.E.2d 284 (Ill. App. 2d Dist. 1967); rev'd Maki v. Frelk, 239 N.E.2d 445 (Ill. 1968).

[10] Since the decision in The Schooner Catharine, 58 U.S. (17 How.) 170 (1854), it has been generally assumed to be the American admiralty rule in col-

tive negligence, apportioning damages between plaintiff and defendant, was developed judicially in Georgia.[11] Moreover, even though a court cannot appropriately lay down some kinds of rules that a legislature might enact, it still seems plain that with choice limited to a rule of no contribution or some rule of contribution within whatever boundaries may be imposed on a court the latter is preferable. A court's view that only the legislature can appropriately lay down the ideal rule should not cause it to adhere to a clearly inferior rule within its own range of choice, except perhaps on a temporary basis in expectation of more sweeping legislative reform. Even this last qualification seems questionable in view of the fact that legislatures respond so seldom and so slowly to needs for reform of tort law.[12]

May we not reasonably challenge, also, the assumption that a court cannot appropriately lay down, through a course of decisions, a system for apportioning damages as finely tailored to the problem as any legislator might draft, including provisions for percentage verdicts, if that be thought wise? Some courts may even now be well on the road to developing such a system.

In pollution cases, wrongdoers formerly were classified as separate and independent tortfeasors rather than joint tortfeasors, with the consequence that often a plaintiff failed to recover anything because he could not prove how much damage each polluter of a stream or lake caused. In recent years, several decisions have imposed joint and sev-

---

lision cases that loss is to be divided equally in cases of contributory fault. But the opinion in that case did not comment on whether that rule should be applied when fault was strikingly unequal, and there have been occasional decisions applying a proportionate-damage rule—for example, The Mary Ida, 20 Fed. 741 (S.D. Ala. 1884). In personal injury claims arising before the Merchant Marine Act of 1920 (Jones Act), § 33, 41 Stat. 1007, 46 U.S.C. § 688 (1958), comparative negligence was an accepted rule, and there was even more support than in collision cases for applying a rule of proportionate damage rather than equal division. In The Max Morris, 137 U.S. 1, 15 (1890), the Supreme Court reserved the question whether damages should be distributed equally or proportionately, and in some cases contributory negligence has been applied in mitigation rather than as a basis for equal division of damages. See The Arizona v. Anelich, 298 U.S. 110, 122 (1936). The history of comparative negligence in English and American admiralty cases is traced in Mole and Wilson, "A Study of Comparative Negligence," pp. 341–347, and Turk, "Comparative Negligence on the March," pp. 226–238, 304.

[11] The doctrine preceded codification. Since codification it has been applied more widely than to the class of cases referred to in the code. See Peck, "Comparative Negligence and Automobile Liability Insurance," pp. 701–702; Turk, "Comparative Negligence on the March," pp. 326–333.

[12] See the comments above, pp. 16–20, regarding legislative inertia and the effect of combined decisional and statutory creativity with respect to immunity doctrines.

eral liability upon contributors of pollution to a stream or lake, and the plaintiff may recover full damages from any one of the polluters.[13] These decisions seem to leave open the possibility, however, that a wrongdoer will be classified not as a joint but as a separate tortfeasor, responsible for part of the damage only, if he can prove his share of the wrong.[14] Thus out of a succession of individual decisions there may be emerging a system of comparative fault under which the innocent plaintiff is entitled to full compensation from any one or more of the tortfeasors he may reach, and among the tortfeasors there is a right of contribution to bring about equal sharing of the loss, except insofar as one or more among the tortfeasors may prove his share of the wrong to be less.

The type of case most conducive to developing such a system is the pollution case, in which the share of the wrong may be approached in terms of the amount of polluting matter discharged by one tortfeasor in comparison with that discharged by others. There are easy steps of analogy, however, to other cases of independent actions of several persons that bring about successive impacts upon the plaintiff,[15] and fi-

[13] For example: Phillips Petroleum Co. v. Hardee, 189 F.2d 205 (5th Cir. 1951) (applying Louisiana law); Landers v. East Texas Salt Water Disposal Co., 151 Tex. 251, 248 S.W.2d 731 (1952) (overruling a precedent that treated the wrongdoers as separate and independent tortfeasors); Annot., 19 A.L.R.2d 1025, 1042–1044 (1951). The weight of authority to the contrary is reviewed in the *Landers* opinion, 151 Tex. at 255, 248 S.W.2d at 733.

[14] Observe the qualification of the court's statement of the rule of decision in *Landers*, 151 Tex. at 256, 248 S.W. 2d at 734: "Where the tortious acts of two or more wrongdoers join to produce an indivisible injury, that is, *an injury which from its nature cannot be apportioned with reasonable certainty to the individual wrongdoers,* all of the wrongdoers will be held jointly and severally liable for the entire damages" (emphasis added). In view of the italicized phrase, might the defendant limit his liability by offering reasonably certain proof that he was responsible for only an identified portion of the harm suffered? If not, might apportionment nevertheless be accomplished through the claim of one tortfeasor against another? On the latter possibility, see "Survey of Southwestern Law for the Year 1952," 7 *SW. L. J.* 330, 400, 404–406 (1953).

Compare Prosser, "Proximate Cause in California," 38 *Calif. L. Rev.* 369, 386–389 (1950), in which Dean Prosser argues that a California precedent similar to that overruled in *Landers* "cannot be accepted as the present law" of California in view of a course of decisions imposing the burden of proof on a defendant, when it is clear he has been at fault, to show the extent of his contribution to the loss or suffer a judgment for the entire amount. See also Prosser, *Torts* (3rd ed. 1964), § 42, p. 253.

[15] Compare Murphy v. Taxicabs of Louisville, Inc., 330 S.W.2d 395 (Ky. 1959). In this case the plaintiff's vehicle was struck twice from the rear. There was one collision involving only the car directly behind him and another involving also a car two vehicles back, and the plaintiff could not prove which impact caused injury. Summary judgment for defendants was reversed on the theory that

48

nally to cases of single impacts in which the proof of shares of the wrong would be developed on a percentage basis comparable to that in some comparative negligence statutes.

The added step to adopting a system of comparative negligence including the plaintiff among those sharing in the loss is only another moderate analogical extension. Thus the extensive development, both statutory and decisional, concerning contribution among tortfeasors works in the direction of undermining the foundation of the doctrine that contributory negligence is a complete bar to recovery. It works in the direction of preparing the way for the final "abrupt" change of overruling this doctrine, as well as vestiges of the doctrine that contribution among tortfeasors is not allowed.

From the point of view of substantive law development, adopting comparative negligence is less of a change than it might appear to be in theory.[16] Among the factors combining to make this the case is the existing unlegitimated practice of juries in applying a rough rule of apportionment.[17]

Jury noncompliance with the rule that contributory negligence bars recovery is also a striking demonstration that this rule is out of keeping with the prevailing sense of justice. The validity of this point is not met by the argument that more legislatures would adopt comparative negligence statutes if this were so. Any proposal for legislation bears a heavy burden of overcoming inertia in the legislative process, and this burden weighs most heavily on proposals for reform of legal doctrine developed in the common law tradition, particularly when the only effective pressure groups available to champion the reform are likely to be especially vulnerable to a charge of acting on self-interest. Nor is the validity of this point met by citation of the Arkansas episode of adoption and later repeal of a broad form of comparative negli-

---

each wrongdoer has the burden of proving his own innocence or limited liability. The decision, however, may have stemmed partly from a Kentucky statute, Ky. Rev. Stat. § 454.040 (1960), authorizing the severance of damages in such a case.

See also Loui v. Oakley, 438 P.2d 393 (Hawaii 1968), allowing rough apportionment by the jury and calling attention to the relationship of this problem to comparative negligence.

[16] See Peck, "Comparative Negligence and Automobile Liability Insurance," concluding that the shift would have little effect, if any, on liability insurance rates. Compare Rosenberg, "Comparative Negligence in Arkansas: A 'Before and After' Survey," 13 *Ark. L. Rev.* 89, 108 (1959), concluding that the shift altered lawyers' evaluations of cases for settlement and caused plaintiffs to win a higher proportion of verdicts, but not larger verdicts.

[17] See below, pp. 74–75.

gence.[18] The repealing statute, rather than returning to the contributory negligence rule, settled on the more limited form of comparative negligence that applies only when the plaintiff's negligence is "of less degree" than the defendant's. Moreover, there are other instances of adoption and adherence to the broader form of comparative negligence,[19] despite the formidable obstacles to legislative reform of legal doctrine.

A second reason that adopting comparative negligence would be a relatively moderate change of substantive law is its consistency with the principle of basing liability on fault. Indeed, comparative negligence is more faithful than the contributory negligence rule to this principle.

Nor is the contemplated action extraordinary from the point of view of legal process. Accomplishing the change to comparative negligence by judicial action would not produce such stress on the principles of stare decisis as is commonly suggested by opponents. As just noted, comparative negligence is more faithful than the contributory negligence rule to the principle of basing liability on fault. Sometimes the objectives that underlie the doctrine of stare decisis—stability, predictability, and evenhandedness of law—are better served by fidelity to principle than by fidelity to specific rules. Moreover, uncertainties and lack of evenhandedness are produced by doctrines of last clear chance, by findings of recklessness made to escape the bar of contributory fault, and by distinctions between what is enough to sustain a finding of primary negligence and what more is required to sustain a finding of contributory negligence. Perhaps even more significant in this respect is the fact that the widespread jury practice of departing from evenhanded application of the legal rules of negligence and contributory negligence produces a kind of rough apportionment of damages, but in an unpoliced, irregular, and unreasonably discriminatory fashion.

By sitting silently by while this element of duplicity extends its corroding influence into attitudes about law and legal institutions, courts are failing to meet their responsibility for remedial action. It is no excuse for courts that legislatures could act if only they would. The responsibility for law reform is not exclusively the task of either. With respect to this specific problem, moreover, courts are at least as well

[18] Ark. Stat. Ann. § § 27-1730.1–2 (Supp. 1961), repealing Ark. Acts 1955, No. 191.
[19] The state of such legislation is reviewed in Peck, "Comparative Negligence and Automobile Liability Insurance," pp. 700–707.

situated as legislatures to inform themselves about all the factors that should be taken into account even for fashioning a new doctrine in full detail and announcing it all at once. They are better situated than legislatures for developing a doctrine of comparative negligence gradually, for a court can resolve questions of detail as they are presented in the context of concrete cases and need not attempt—to the extent a legislature does—to anticipate questions and answer them in advance.

Thus, stability, predictability, and evenhandedness are better served by judicial adoption of comparative negligence than by judicial adherence in theory to a law that contributory fault bars when this rule has ceased to be the law in action.

Retroactive overruling seems appropriate in these circumstances.[20] Some will disagree with this conclusion on the ground that, in its practical impact on claims, disparity between the present unlegitimated system and a candid system of comparative negligence is greater than suggested here; they may urge that retroactive overruling would cause substantial disappointment of expectations arising from reliance on the old rule, either in the determination of liability insurance rates or otherwise. To meet such objections, there remains the technique of prospective overruling. Also—in view of the current difficulty of obtaining majority assent to either retroactive or prospective overruling of the contributory negligence doctrine—there will no doubt be opportunities in most jurisdictions for expressing the need for reform in concurring and dissenting opinions.

A judge who accepts the views expressed here and is prepared to overrule retroactively might appropriately write an opinion that proceeds, in outline, as follows.

"The rule that contributory negligence is a complete bar, if ever a wise doctrine, was supportable only under circumstances that no longer exist in our economic, social, and political environment. Though its foundation is a premise of liability based on fault, it departs from an implication of that premise by visiting an entire accidental loss on one of the parties whose negligent conduct combined to cause it. The same is true of any qualification of the rule of contributory negligence, such as the doctrine of last clear chance, that shifts the entire loss rather than shifting none of it. It is also true of the analogous rule against contribution among tortfeasors. Recognition of that inconsistency with the premise of liability based on fault has doubtless been a significant

---

[20] See Warren A. Seavey, *Cogitations on Torts* (1954), pp. 55–57.

factor in the statutory and decisional trend toward contribution—a trend compatible with a principle of apportionment. Moreover, the rule of contributory negligence is so out of keeping with the prevailing thought of the community that to a very considerable degree it has been vitiated by verdicts that in effect apply a rule of apportionment in direct opposition to jury instructions—a situation that promotes disrespect for law and legal institutions.

"A principle of comparative fault, involving apportionment of the loss among the several negligent contributors to its occurrence, is more consistent with the premise of liability based on fault. It is also a preferable rule from the point of view of its practical impact upon claims for compensation of losses arising from accidental injury. In short, it is, in the view of those joining in this opinion, a far better approach to justice in cases of this type than the current doctrine. It should therefore be adopted, and the doctrine that contributory negligence is a complete bar to recovery should be overruled."

If the opinion is that of a minority, it might appropriately remain silent on the issue of prospective versus retroactive overruling, since inherently a dissenting or concurring opinion gives notice of the doubtful reliability of the old doctrine in the future. If it is a majority opinion, however, that choice must be faced. If most of the members of a court accept the desirability of reform but, because of concern about expectations arising from reliance on the old rule, prefer not to overrule retroactively, they might extend their majority opinion in the following vein.

"In view of the long and firm acceptance of the rule of contributory negligence in the decisions of this jurisdiction and the possibility of substantial interests arising from reliance on the old rule, objections are raised to retroactive overruling. In deference to such objections, those members of the court who join in this opinion do not favor overruling retroactively in the present case. But the doctrine of contributory negligence as a complete bar is hereby overruled prospectively and a principle of apportionment of damages is adopted in its stead. Subsidiary questions concerned with precise formulation of the doctrine of apportionment are left to future determination as they are presented."

The case for overruling the contributory negligence doctrine is compelling. Why, then, has no court of last resort yet acted, even in a decade when the spirit of change has been strong? Perhaps the obstacle thus far insurmountable has been the notion that only a legislature

should change a rule of such pervasive impact as the contributory negligence rule. It is true, of course, that as the scope of a rule's applicability is greater, so is the significance of change. But so, too, is the
urgency of the need for change. It is not alone around the rough edges
of the law of torts that legislative inertia can defeat justice.

As judges and critics develop, side-by-side, generalized principles
and particularized rules for determining whether courts should on a
particular occasion exercise their admitted power to overrule precedents, and if so in what way, the accumulated guidance will make less
difficult both the problem of distinguishing appropriate from inappropriate occasions for overruling precedents and the choice among methods. One consequence should be that more courts will be persuaded to
join in the task of law reform.

Chapter 4

Evolutionary Revision of Legal Doctrine in Courts

*T*HE GREATER part of the creative contribution of courts to law reform comes about in an unspectacular way. This continued to be the case even during the decade commencing in 1958, when, in comparison with other periods of equal length, the most distinctive aspect of appellate court performance was the rising tide of overruling decisions. A greater contribution, even then, occurred in the day-to-day development of legal doctrine in ways short of overruling precedents.

On the whole, courts are performing a greater share of the burden of law reform than legislatures, even though legislatures have greater freedom in making abrupt changes, and even though the creative work of courts is more often in adjusting, adapting, and elaborating segments of doctrine than in overruling. Decisional creativity is a more potent instrument of reform than statutory creativity. Curiously, this result has been brought about by a combination of judicial assertiveness and judicial restraint—assertiveness in aversion to legislation as alien to the common law,[1] perhaps more marked in the early part of the twentieth century than in recent years, and restraint about presuming to apply a statute beyond the letter of its coverage (even when such interpretation is essential to achieving an apparent legislative purpose).[2] A judicial decision overruling a precedent is commonly a significant, continuing force for law reform as its implications are pursued and its influence is extended by analogy. But courts are more reluctant, almost to the point of abstention, about reasoning by analogy from a statute or extending its principle to situations not dealt with explicitly or by clear implication in the statutory formulation.[3]

[1] See Pound, "Common Law and Legislation," 21 *Harv. L. Rev.* 383, 385 (1908).

[2] See Pound, *Jurisprudence* (1959), III, 654–671; Landis, "Statutes and the Sources of Law," in *Harvard Legal Essays* (1934), pp. 213, 217.

[3] See, for example, Landis, p. 221; Schaefer, *Precedent and Policy* (1956), pp. 15–19.

CONCEPTUALISM AND MANIPULATION OF DOCTRINE

That doctrine can be so radically changed in an evolutionary way is at once strength and weakness, armor and vulnerability. Misunderstandings of this characteristic of legal doctrine, advanced perhaps as often by misguided partisans of the splendor of decisional doctrine as by its detractors, account for the fact that legal doctrine is sometimes held in extraordinarily low esteem. Those who express great admiration for legal doctrine but see in every creative judicial decision a threat to the integrity of the judicial process do great disservice by contributing to an image of doctrine as a system of concepts designed to move with logical precision to a foreordained result, a bulwark against both uncertainty and change. This image is acceptable to those who, in the hope of advancing the cause of needed reform, wish doctrine to be seen as the dead hand of the past. Among a remarkable number of persons who recognize needs for law reform, avowed reliance upon doctrine is branded as "conceptualism"—if not dealt with more harshly— and treated as a skeleton in the closet.

The practice to which the term conceptualism refers deserves its state of disrepute if that term is understood not broadly and descriptively as any systematic use of concepts, but narrowly and normatively as casuistry. Perhaps this is the common usage. But the severest critics of conceptualism in the law, though conceding some place to doctrine as the language of the law—as a medium for expressing decisions reached on other grounds—have condemned efforts to use doctrine in aid of decision itself. They have urged that courts should be free to work out just or fair or acceptable results in particular cases without the frustrating inconvenience of doctrinal limitations. Others, somewhat less sanguine in their criticism, have asserted that commonly, at least, doctrinal reasoning in judicial opinions is a facade for other grounds of decision that could not be stated—that legal concepts, serving as only a means for achieving justice, are tools to be manipulated to attain results chosen by other tests.

The nature of partisan reactions to doctrinal changes may seem to lend credit to the view that doctrines are only manipulative tools. For example, on the one hand, an opinion expanding liability is referred to as "masterly" and is credited with leveling "the withering fire of . . . unsparing analysis" at "the flawed and fallible privity rule" in the area

55

of products liability.[4] On the other hand, the same case is referred to as one of three that "were enshrouded in an emotional atmosphere" by which the courts "were compelled 'to do justice' at the expense of long-established legal principles."[5] Another opinion of the same court, *Botta v. Brunner,*[6] denying to plaintiff's counsel the privilege of suggesting either an amount or a mathematical formula in his argument to the jury concerning damages for pain and suffering, and expressly overruling precedents that were "to some degree" in conflict with this view, predictably reverses the positions of partisan commentators. It is referred to by the critics on the plaintiffs' side as "dubious," "benighted," "lamentable," and contrary to "the modern weight of authority."[7] Defense partisans call it "a masterpiece of sound thinking and judicial writing."[8]

In the din of such clashing comments are overtones concerning creativity and continuity. It happens that the dominant trend of creativity in tort law, despite occasional episodes of reversion[9] and occasional exceptions such as *Botta,* has been one of expanding liability. This trend was an aftermath of the idea that there should be no recovery unless an action could be brought within one of the writs—an idea that gave overwhelming emphasis to continuity. In the recent past the trend of expanding liability has accelerated under the influence of changing economic and social attitudes. Other factors of less pervasive significance have also made their contribution. For example, fear that the courts would be overwhelmed with insoluble problems if a proposed area of liability were recognized produced in tort law a considerable body of rules that cut corners to achieve simplicity and ease of administration. With increasing confidence in the capacity of the legal system to master difficult questions of fact, courts have warmed to the task of

[4] Lambert, "The Common Law: Steadfast and Changing," 25 *NACCA L. J.* 25, 30 (1960), referring to Henningsen v. Bloomfield Motors, Inc., 32 N.J. 358, 161 A.2d 69 (1960).

[5] Freedman, *Products Liability—The Three-Pronged Sword of Damocles: Cutter, Henningsen, and Greenberg* (undated monograph of the Defense Research Institute, published in 1961), p. 2.

[6] 26 N.J. 82, 138 A.2d 713 (1958).

[7] Lambert, "Comments on Recent Important Personal Injury (Tort) Cases," 25 *NACCA L. J.* 47, 68 (1960).

[8] 4 *Defense L. J.* 288, 289 (1958).

[9] Nineteenth century development of the law of negligence, in contrast with liability in some degree stricter in earlier common law, is commonly regarded as such an episode.

developing in such areas—particularly those concerned with mental suffering and privacy—rules more finely tailored to doing justice in cases formerly beyond the exclusionary line.

Thus under various influences creativity has continued to be the favorite of the plaintiffs' bar and stability the favorite of their opposition. But *Botta* may well prove to be a forerunner of more extended controversy over doctrines concerned with the assessment of damages. In such a context, creativity will be pleasing sometimes to plaintiffs [10] and at other times to defendants. One can imagine that if a court should decide to deny or to limit allowances for pain and suffering in a previously unfamiliar way "the bromidic contention of habitual defendants that, if an immunity is to be abolished, it must be done by the legislature, not by the court" would be borrowed and adapted by the plaintiffs' partisans; in turn, the defendants' partisans would embrace the view that a court that opened its doors without legislative help can likewise close them.[11]

Such partisan reactions as these must be appraised as manifestations of advocacy. The role of the advocate demands that he examine doctrine from a point of view based on the premise that the interest he represents should prevail. Thus in a sense he engages in manipulation; he formulates doctrinal arguments to sustain positions he adopts because of his commitment to an outside, partisan premise. But the work of a careful advocate, when he is directing his attention to persuading a court rather than merely to stimulating enthusiasm among partisans, reflects a sensitivity to the obligation of the court to reach principled decisions—decisions that not only are reasoned but also are grounded on premises of nonpartisan character.[12] The practices of advocacy,

[10] See Wycko v. Gnodtke, 361 Mich. 331, 105 N.W.2d 118 (1960), construing in an expansive way, contrary to precedents, the statutory provision for damages on account of the death of a minor.

[11] The quotation and a statement of the opposing argument paraphrased here appear in Lambert, "The Common Law: Steadfast and Changing," pp. 25–26.

[12] Compare Wechsler, "Toward Neutral Principles of Constitutional Law," 73 *Harv. L. Rev.* 1, 19 (1959) reprinted in *Principles, Politics, and Fundamental Law*, p. 27 (1961). Wechsler observes that in relation to constitutional issues a court is bound to function not as a naked power organ but by decisions that are principled in the sense of resting on "reasons that in their generality and their neutrality transcend any immediate result that is involved." His full development of this idea is associated with the obligation, in relation to constitutional issues, of judicial restraint in overriding choices of other branches of the government. The point that it is a court's duty to function by principled decision seems equally applicable, however, to other legal issues.

then, do not constitute a denial of the usefulness of doctrine as a guide to principled decision. Nevertheless, partisan manipulation has made its contribution to skepticism about legal doctrine.

Another cause for skepticism about legal doctrine has been its imperfection both in guiding decisions and in reflecting the real grounds on which they are based.

A judicial opinion is ordinarily written in a style of conviction even though grave doubt has beset its author along the road of deliberation and drafting. Greater doubt, still, may lie in the minds of other members of the court who acquiesce—doubt that remains unexpressed because dissents and concurrences are ordinarily inspired by conviction, not doubt. Moreover, the influences that have brought conviction, to the extent it exists, are imperfectly perceived by the judge himself and could not be fully discovered even by the most thorough inquiry into his conscious and subconscious processes. Thus even a court whose every member is committed to the ideal of judicial opinions that express in candor the convictions reached and the grounds that were persuasive will yet fail to produce any opinion that attains the ideal.[13] Elusiveness of the ideal, however, is no proof that striving toward it is either abnormal or unwise. We may never strike the center of the target, but we shall more often strike near it by aiming there.

SOUND USES OF LEGAL DOCTRINE

Though choices must be made with respect to methods of deciding cases and writing opinions, there is no choice between use and nonuse of doctrinal aids to decision—conceptual aids, if you please. Rather, the choices are concerned with finding ways of wisely using and developing them. Every system of reasoned thought must have its basis in concepts. Adherence of a legal system to stability, predictability, and continuity is adherence to a form of conceptualism, in the broad sense. The use of concepts is dictated by the election of reason as a guide to decision in preference to pure hunch. Nor can concepts be assigned merely the role of a medium for after-the-fact explanation of decisions reached on unexplained grounds; the goal is reasoned judgments, not merely reasoned explanations.

Legal doctrines are also essential devices for insuring equality of treatment by the host of people who make final dispositions of particu-

[13] The points summarized in this paragraph have been developed by a distinguished appellate justice in Schaefer, *Precedent and Policy*, pp. 5–8, 20.

lar disputes. The number of such persons is not exhausted in the tally of those having official roles of adjudication. It has been estimated that not more than 2 or 3 percent of potential personal injury claims, for example, proceed to a trial-court judgment; [14] a much smaller percentage of cases reaches any court of last resort. Moreover, despite the most assiduous efforts at maintaining a system of decision by rule of law, in contrast with decision by the exercise of unlimited personal discretion, there exists a considerable practice of forum shopping to take advantage of the known tendencies of particular courts and judges. This is an inevitable characteristic of any set of institutions for resolving disputes. The system that is commonly referred to as the rule of law, and the use of doctrine that is an essential part of it, are instruments for keeping this arbitrary element in narrow bounds.

A common criticism of judicial performance sets policy considerations against doctrine, realism against conceptualism, and functional analysis against legal analysis. It relegates legal concepts and doctrine to the level of technical manipulative instruments for implementing the social goals chosen by policy and functional analysis. This purported confrontation is false, and it remains so whatever the labels may be.[15]

In the first place, every doctrine has its foundations in policy considerations of one kind or another, whether explicit or not. Perhaps stare decisis is the doctrine most maligned by those who blame judicial views about legal doctrine for the sluggishness of legal institutions in responding to needs for reform. But even stare decisis has firm support in policy. It is a doctrine concerned with preserving the continuity essential to fair and efficient adjudication and to guiding private conduct in reliance upon law.[16] When the issue is whether a well-established doctrine shall be overruled, the confrontation is not one between the

---

[14] "On the average, in the United States only about one fifth of all personal injury claims are ever filed in court, only about 5 per cent ever reach the trial stage, and only 2 or 3 per cent ever reach the stage where they are decided by the verdict of a jury or the judgment of a court." Hans Zeisel, Harry Kalven, and Bernard Buchholz, *Delay in the Court* (1959), p. 105. The definitions of "claim" on which available data are based and the selective sources of data affect this percentage (see *ibid.*, p. 114 and n. 6). Perhaps a corrected figure would be on the lower side of the range of 2 or 3 percent.

[15] The attempt at separation of "is" and "ought"—the fallacy of which is developed in Lon L. Fuller, *The Law in Quest of Itself* (1940)—is quite similar to this attempt at separation of "doctrine" and "policy," although some of the detractors of doctrine would identify the law that "is" with decisional results and official actions rather than with doctrine, leaving the latter in limbo as neither "is" nor "ought."

[16] See Hart and Sacks, *The Legal Process* (Tent. ed. 1958), pp. 587–588.

doctrine of stare decisis and meritorious policy considerations. Rather, the confrontation is concerned partly with the respective merits that the old and the proposed doctrine would have if the lawmaker were writing on a clean slate, partly with the modifications of that appraisal that are incident to the existence of an established doctrine, partly with preserving a firm tradition of evenhanded continuity, and partly with maintaining a capacity for creative development in law.

The full association of doctrine and policy is not represented adequately by the figure of speech that declares doctrine to be founded on policy considerations. The policy considerations are interwoven into the fabric of the doctrine itself. One who undertakes to interpret doctrine and to apply it independently of attention to the policy considerations that are associated with its creative decisional development misunderstands the doctrine itself.

Thus, to argue for an interpretation or elaboration of doctrine beyond the particularized rules it has produced, in order to serve the policy considerations found to be implicit in the doctrine and its particularized rules, is to argue not for revision but for fulfillment of the doctrine itself. An example is the gradual elaboration of rules denying privity requirements in various particularized contexts, in the years following the decision in *MacPherson v. Buick Motor Co.*[17] The majority in that case explicitly announced a principle of responsibility of manufacturers for foreseeable injuries resulting from negligently made products, and referred to policy considerations supporting the principle. Yet their opinion was cautiously conservative about details. For instance, the stated criterion for foreseeable injuries was narrower than the reasons stated to support it. And the opinion explicitly reserved judgment about the liability of a manufacturer of a component part of the retail product, though the reasoning used in sustaining liability against the assembler of the automobile seems equally forceful against the maker of the wheel that failed. An astute lawyer advising a client after this opinion was rendered would at the least have called his attention to a possibility, and perhaps even a high probability, of the New York court's developing both a more inclusive formulation of the criterion for foreseeable injuries and a rule subjecting manufacturers of component parts to liability similar to that imposed on the assembler by this decision. The later decisions in which these developments occurred were, then, the fulfillment of the doctrine of *MacPherson* rather than a revision of that doctrine.

[17] 217 N.Y. 382, 111 N.E.1050 (1916).

This is not to say, however, that all evolutionary development of decisional doctrine is fulfillment of the implications of the doctrine itself as it stood at some earlier point in time. Indeed, much of the evolutionary development is truly revision rather than fulfillment. Consider *Mac-Pherson* again, but this time from the perspective of its consistency with antecedents rather than sequels. *MacPherson* changed the law, even though the majority opinion did not purport to overrule any precedent. To us, in a later generation, it may seem that it would have been better to overrule candidly than to initiate less openly such a pregnant departure in principle. But the fact remains that the method used was to array all the recognized exceptions to the privity requirement and to declare, for the first time officially at least, an organizing principle that encompassed them all. This was a new departure in principle and in policy, but through the technique of evolutionary revision of doctrine rather than the technique of overruling.

MacPherson illustrates that the policy considerations affecting evolution of legal doctrine are not limited to those interwoven into the doctrine as it stands at some chosen point in time. Rather, legal doctrine may be criticized on policy grounds beyond those it recognizes, and it may in time be revised because such criticisms have found their mark. Thus, legal doctrine is always subject to reasoned evaluation on policy grounds, including policy arguments expressly or impliedly rejected by the doctrine as well as those expressly or impliedly interwoven into its fabric. The true confrontation, however, is not between policy and doctrine but between policy and policy.

The confrontation is in fact even more subtle and less sharply defined than is implied in speaking of it merely as a confrontation between policy and policy. For it is not often a confrontation simply of one policy against another policy, a confrontation in which one policy must be accepted and the other rejected. Rather the relevant policies are many, and among them are policies in varying degrees consistent and inconsistent, competing and reinforcing. Partly because considerations commonly referred to as policy arguments are ordinarily relatively general in character, formulations expressed solely in terms of policies often prove to be unserviceable as guides to decision. More particularized formulations of doctrine represent efforts at crystallizing appraisals of a variety of policy considerations into a relatively firm guide to decision.

But it is rare, especially in the law of torts, that such firmness reaches the point of rigidity. It is an everyday occurrence for courts to examine the more specific formulations of a doctrine in light of the broader considerations associated with its development, seeking the sense of the doctrine in relation to a current problem, or even the sense of apparently competing doctrines each of which might be extended by analogy to the current problem. Moreover, there are ordinarily cumulative policy considerations on both sides of any seriously disputed issue, and the decisions that courts reach are the consequence of weighing these competing considerations.[18] No single policy reason is alone a satisfactory explanation of the pattern of decisions that emerges. Relentless pursuit of the logical implications of a single policy reason is usually a distortion of the legal doctrine expressed and implicit in a succession of related decisions.

The doctrine does not foreordain the court's conclusion. The court is exercising a choice—a choice, however, that is to be exercised not blindly or arbitrarily but responsibly,[19] and under the guidance of reason and an accumulation of ideas that are expressed or implied in legal doctrine with varying shades of clarity.[20]

In part, controversy over the role of doctrine may be traced to preferences concerning ways of describing the continually creative role of courts in day-to-day work. If one chooses to treat separately the law that "is" from the law that "is becoming," defining doctrine in a static sense and viewing nondoctrinal considerations as the real grounds of decision, he is then confronted with the choice of either picturing doctrine as a facade or else negating his own separation by conceding that doctrine itself serves as a guide to recognizing and appraising the considerations that are decisive. Attempts at separating the doctrinal from the real grounds of decision understate the role of doctrine in relation to both creativity and guidance of decision and overstate the incidence in our legal system of that kind of duplicity that is inherent in deviation between real and stated reasons. Insistence on separating doctrinal

[18] Compare Smith, "Cumulative Reasons and Legal Method," 27 *Texas L. Rev.* 454, 458–459, 468 (1949).

[19] Cooperrider, "The Rule of Law and the Judicial Process," 59 *Mich. L. Rev.* 501, 513 (1961), comments that the "judge who has discovered the freedom and the power which are his should be chastened rather than elated by the discovery. It is possible to harbor this knowledge without deriving from it the conclusion that the judge should convert himself into a ruler, a manipulator of those who have reposed in him a very special trust." Though this quotation is in harmony with the views expressed here, Cooperrider's article as a whole appears to favor a role for courts that gives somewhat greater emphasis to continuity and somewhat less to creativity than this book is intended to support.

[20] Compare Cardozo, *The Growth of the Law* (1924), pp. 58–64.

and actual grounds of decision seems more likely to mislead than to enlighten, more likely to discourage with cynicism than to encourage with hope the commitment of intellectual energies to the task of improving decisional law.

A major portion of the judiciary's creative contribution to law revision will continue to be made in evolutionary rather than overruling decisions. Candid recognition that doctrinal evolution is a blend between fulfillment and revision of the policies interwoven into legal doctrine will aid in focusing attention and debate upon the issues that ought to be decisive, case by case, as this evolutionary process continues.

Chapter 5

Juries and Trial Judges as Agencies of Law Reform and Administration

*C*OURTS function under an obligation of principled decision, and this obligation implies constraints. Essential as they are to regularity of process, such limits are nonetheless certain to be controversial. Even among those who see wisely designed constraints as the essence of good process—the key to just results in the maximum percentage of cases—there may be sharp differences about the efficacy of particular checks. We have seen examples of such differences in the varied attitudes toward overruling precedents.

The constraints essential to regularity of process are, from another point of view, rules allocating responsibility for decision. For example, restrictions against a judge's overturning a jury verdict allocate to the jury a large measure of responsibility for deciding issues of disputed fact. Conversely, restrictions against a jury's rendering a verdict contrary to the evidence allocate to the judge a responsibility for deciding whether the jury verdict is beyond the permissible range.

Every rule of substantive law functions in some measure as a constraint and conversely as an element of the allocation of responsibility for decision among judges, juries, and any other agencies participating in the process of adjudication. But the degree of constraint that may seem superficially to be implicit in a rule of substantive law is sharply reduced if the enforcement of the rule is entrusted to an agency whose decision is largely free from re-examination. The prime example of such an agency is the jury. And, not surprisingly, even among those who believe most strongly in the efficacy of jury trial, there is controversy about the proper limits of the jury's unfettered discretion.

One technique for entrusting discretion to any legal institution, including juries, is to formulate the constraints—the guiding directives—in generalized rather than particularized legal doctrine. The result is not merely freedom to act in ways that defy orderly classification but also freedom to develop patterns of customary action, as juries have done in some matters. There is freedom also to change those patterns, and juries have done so with changing public attitudes.

64

Thus the degree of generality of legal doctrine has an important impact on law reform. One method of reforming law, often used but less often acknowledged, is to commit questions to juries and trial judges under very generalized doctrines within whose loosely policed expanses reform can proceed undercover.

GENERALITY OF DOCTRINE IN ITS GUIDING QUALITY

In direct relation to the progression from generality to particularity of doctrine in its guiding quality is the progression from the discretionary to the ministerial in its application. If a doctrine establishes a comparatively general standard of judgment, one who applies the standard to the individual case exercises a high degree of discretion. Such discretionary decisions are often referred to as factfindings when the function of making them is allocated between judge and jury in much the same way as the function of deciding issues of physical fact. But this type of factfinding is in truth a judgment of an evaluative character rather than a finding that some physical event did or did not occur. On the other hand, if a doctrine establishes a comparatively particular rule for guiding decisions, applying the rule as distinguished from finding physical facts is essentially ministerial.

Consider, for example, the problem of consent by a young person to a medical operation. If tort doctrine makes the effectiveness of expressions of consent turn upon application of a general standard concerned with whether the person consenting has the capacity to understand the nature of the proposed intrusion upon his person and the risks involved,[1] it calls for a discretionary decision—an evaluation—even though it may be called a factfinding. If, in contrast, tort doctrine makes the effectiveness of expressions of consent turn on whether the person consenting has reached the age of twenty-one years,[2] it calls for a physical factfinding of age, readily determinable in most cases, and

[1] See, for example, Gulf & S.I.R.R. v. Sullivan, 155 Miss. 1, 119 So. 501 (1929) (consent of seventeen-year-old to vaccination held a bar to his suit since he had sufficient intelligence to understand and appreciate the consequences); *Restatement (Second), Torts,* § 59 (1965); *Restatement, Torts,* § 892 (1939).

[2] See, for example, Bonner v. Moran, 126 F.2d 121 (D.C. Cir. 1941) (consent by fifteen-year-old boy to operation, in which he was a skin-graft donor for the benefit of a cousin, held ineffectual; suggestions that consent of a parent may be required until the child reaches the age of twenty-one, though a ground of decision of the instant case was that the operation was for the benefit of another rather than the consenting minor).

65

with perhaps a few exceptions [3] only a ministerial application of the rule.

A full description of the basis of judgment in an individual case to which a doctrinal formulation of relatively general guiding quality applies is in another sense very particular in character. That is, it is likely to be tailored peculiarly to the specific case, within the wide leeway allowed by the doctrinal formulation. There is no obligation to disclose details of the basis of the judgment worked out within that leeway. Thus there is no technique available for causing the same basis of judgment to be applied in other cases as well. The doctrinal formulation that is relatively general with respect to its guiding quality produces individual applications that are quite particular in the sense of freedom from policing to insure that the basis of judgment is not peculiar. Thus the doctrinal formulations of relatively general guiding quality are most likely to be offensive to evenhandedness in the sense of consistent application of a single basis for decision of cases that fall within a type identified by the doctrinal formulation.

It has become customary to refer to the doctrinal formulations of particularized guiding quality (like the age-of-twenty-one formulation) as rules and to the formulations of generalized guiding quality (like the age-of-understanding formulation) as standards.[4] Undoubtedly both of these kinds of doctrine are useful in a legal system. Some issues are best dealt with by providing for a relatively wide discretion at the level of application. It has not been possible in all instances to develop a formulation with particularized guidelines of rational rather than arbitrary character. Moreover, a doctrine allowing discretion in its application to particular cases has the advantages of flexibility at the level of first instance, where the institutions for adjudication come into closest association with the litigants and the facts and where far the greater percentage of litigated controversies are terminated. Such flexi-

[3] For example, the definition of "the age of twenty-one years" may produce difficulty in cases close to the dividing line. Compare property law problems of this type adverted to in Leach, "The Careful Draftsman: Watch Out!" 47 *A.B.A.J.* 259 (1961).

[4] Compare Pound, *Jurisprudence*, II, 124–128. The usage suggested here is not precisely that formulated by Dean Pound. He defines a standard as "a measure of conduct prescribed by law from which one departs at his peril of answering for resulting damage or of legal invalidity of what he does" (p. 127), whereas the somewhat broader usage suggested here includes a measure of capacity as well as a measure of conduct. With respect to the distinction between particularity of rules and generality of standards as to guiding quality, however, these usages are consistent.

bility allows a nicer weighing of factors of the individual case that might be thought relevant to judgment. But flexibility reduces the degree of consistency among different judgments, even among those of a single adjudicator and far more among those of different adjudicators. To achieve a greater measure of consistency and evenhandedness, it is quite useful to have doctrinal formulations expressed in terms of results reached in relatively particularized types of cases, together with grounds of distinction from other particularized types in which the results reached are different.

Fine tailoring of justice to the individual case may be in some degree sacrificed in order to gain the predictability that is needed for society to function with only occasional resort to litigation and with a reasonable degree of certainty about the legal consequences of what is done.

Even when rules are quite fully particularized and well accepted, however, they are subject to being tested against concepts of more generalized character, described in a variety of ways as principles, policy considerations, economic and social implications, factors of practical import, and so on. Often the more generalized thought remains in the background, receiving no explicit consideration in the doctrinal formulations or in the opinions in which they are evolved. Especially is this true in repeated applications of settled doctrinal formulations. The emphasis in such areas is heavily upon thinking in categories and hardly at all upon appraising the more generalized considerations that have led to development of these categories. But occasionally, especially in developing and disputed areas of law, the more generalized considerations are brought to the foreground and are explicitly relied upon in testing and reaffirming, modifying, or abandoning the more particular, categorical formulations. The interplay of the general and the particular, of the rules and the reasons, is essential to an ideal accommodation of creativity and continuity, and it is desirable that it occur openly in judicial opinions.

Serviceability of a doctrinal formulation as a guide to decision depends on characteristics that may usefully be approached through the following questions: (1) How effectively does the formulation provide a way of determining the scope of its application—a way, aside from the exercise of unarticulated discretionary judgment, of characterizing individual cases as falling within or outside the type and subtypes it establishes? (2) How well does the formulation indicate the legal consequences to be attached to the type and subtypes within its structure?

(3) How well does the formulation indicate reasons associated with its development, an understanding of which will be needed for wise use of the formulation as a guide to decision whenever areas of doubt are confronted? Appraisal of the merits of a doctrinal formulation depends also on two further questions: (4) Are deficiencies of the formulation as a guide to particular decisions unavoidable because of the nature of the problem of judgment to which the doctrinal formulation is addressed; if not, are they nevertheless a reasonable price to pay for advantages inherent in allowing at the level of particular applications a range of unexplained choice—a range of discretion? (5) Is the formulation wisely tailored with respect to its practical import in human affairs and its consistency with community views of fairness, insofar as they can be perceived?[5]

A doctrinal formulation is ill suited to guiding decisions unless all of the first three of these questions can be answered in an affirmative way. For example, developed legal doctrine is rather specific in spinning out the consequences of characterizing a case as within a type involving physical injuries caused to the plaintiff by a servant of the defendant acting within the scope of employment. But the doctrine of the master-servant cases remains a relatively poor guide to decision in a large number of cases because the guides to characterizing the individual case as within or outside this type are quite general. The customary formulation has become one that sets forth a general test—so general that it affords no substantial guidance—and supplements it by declaring that in applying this test to the facts of a particular case one must consider a number of specified factors.[6]

Particularized formulations score higher than the generalized on at least the first two of the tests of serviceability suggested above. Generalized formulations, on the other hand, appear in their most useful role when the nature of the case requires a weighing of competing interests

[5] Compare Llewellyn, *The Common Law Tradition—Deciding Appeals* (1960), p. 335: "The best of them [rules of law] are relatively clear as to whether and when they apply; the best of them are shrewdly tailored to significant types of problem-situation; the best of them carry, also, their reason on their face. Such rules, we have seen, furnish to court and to counsel as much of reasonable regularity, as much of guidance, as is healthy for any living legal system."

[6] See *Restatement (Second), Agency*, §§ 220, 229 (1958). Section 220(2) lists ten "matters of fact" that, "among others," are to be considered in "determining whether one acting for another is a servant or an independent contractor." Section 229(2) lists ten "matters of fact" that are to be considered in "determining whether or not the conduct, although not authorized, is nevertheless so similar to or incidental to the conduct authorized as to be within the scope of employment."

peculiarly dependent on the distinctive facts of the particular case. It is here that the advantages of flexibility are most apparent, allowing a nicer weighing of all the relevant factors of the particular case. The standard for finding negligence in a motoring case is an example—a standard that requires a weighing of utility of particular conduct in a particular context against risks caused by that conduct in that context. One may be critical of the choice that makes liability depend upon negligence, and grounds of criticism may include the fact that the nature of the negligence issue makes it impossible to formulate enough particularized rules to escape the use of a generalized standard for guiding the finding of negligence. But given the decision that negligence is crucial to liability, the strong orientation of the issue toward the facts of each particular case adds cogency to the argument for using a generalized standard, allowing a range of relatively unguided choice in the application of that standard to a set of facts.

Support for using very generalized standards in negligence cases can be found, too, in the fact that efforts to devise detailed rules that govern such findings are likely to produce casuistic refinements not rationally related to the evaluation in each particular case. In such circumstances, it is better to acknowledge the nature of the issue and formulate the standard of evaluation in terms that at least focus attention on the central problem.

A third factor supporting use of the generalized standard in some contexts, including negligence cases, is the difficulty of separating the evaluative issue from the issue of physical fact. This is not to say that supervision of evaluative findings is futile, or that no rules are useful on an issue such as negligence. In fact, to a considerable degree effective supervision is possible, a point that will be considered shortly. Also, the general standard for negligence is qualified by a number of specific rules, particularly those concerned with distinctive groups of persons and those concerned with violation of statutory regulations of conduct. But the area within which such rules can be developed is a limited phase of the total negligence issue, and that issue remains an appropriate one for the generalized standard of judgment, with supplementary arrangements for supervising individual applications of the standard.

SUPERVISION OF CASE DISPOSITIONS

The degree of guidance to decisions at the trial level and the degree of consistency maintained among all case dispositions depend not only upon the generality of doctrinal formulations as to guiding quality but also upon the extent to which applications to particular cases are supervised.

When the nature of the standard of judgment is one that defies particularized formulation, a considerable degree of consistency and predictability of decisions may nevertheless be attained if the court of last resort exercises close supervision. This can be true even if the issue is strongly fact oriented—strongly dependent on the detailed facts of the particular case at hand.

The issue of legal cause in negligence cases is an example. Widely varied doctrinal formulations have been advanced. None of the formulations has served effectively in guiding particular decisions because all have been concerned in one way or another with a concept of risk as an influence on the scope of liability, and that concept is strongly fact oriented. Yet one who studies the decisions of a court of last resort on a succession of legal-cause issues and gives particular attention to fact types can acquire a sense of the concept of risk that runs through the decisions; he can predict reasonably well the decisions of that court in other cases. It is true that because of influences not doctrinally legitimated the degree of predictability of the final result may vary among the cases that are left to jury determination. But one can predict reasonably well whether the court of last resort will determine that the issue of legal cause is to be left to a jury or is to be decided by the court on the ground that reasonable and fair-minded men, correctly understanding the doctrinal formulation, could reach but one conclusion.

As an aid to this kind of prediction, the usefulness of previous decisions on which the forecaster relies depends heavily on close factual similarity. Suppose a precedent involving negligence in allowing sheep to escape into territory fraught with dangers significantly different from those to which they were subject while in their pen. This precedent may be quite useful to one who attempts a prediction concerning another case involving the escape of domestic animals, but it is not very useful in predicting whether the court will allow a jury to find that negligence of a motorist in bringing about a collision was a legal cause of a second collision that occurred when another motorist struck one of the disabled vehicles ten minutes later. This remains true even if the doctrinal formulations of legal cause applied in the two cases are identical.

Thus in their practical impact the nature of doctrinal guides with respect to generality—with respect to the degree of discretion allowed at the level of application to particular cases—depends both on the particularity or generality of the verbal formulation and on the extent to which the verbal formulation is or is not clarified in meaning by appellate supervision of its application to particular cases. It would be unrealistic to suppose that the appellate guidance of decisions on legal cause remains substantially the same today as at a time decades past, merely on evidence that the verbal formulation of the applicable doctrine continues to be substantially the same.

THE FUNCTION OF MAKING EVALUATIVE FINDINGS

A system for supervising application of a relatively general doctrinal formulation to particular cases must answer the question whether the function of making evaluative findings essential to the application is to be treated as a question for the factfinder, usually the jury, or a question for judges in their more narrowly defined judicial role. It is plain that the evaluative finding that characterizes conduct as negligent or not is to be made by the factfinder, with certainly no more and perhaps somewhat less judicial supervision than that over findings of physical fact. In some other areas of tort law, however, it appears to be the settled law that the function of evaluative finding is entirely judicial. These are illustrations: (1) the characterization of conduct as falling within the principle of *Rylands v. Fletcher*[7] where that principle is recognized, or as being ultrahazardous or abnormally dangerous;[8] (2) in the law of malicious prosecution the characterization of grounds for instigating criminal proceedings as amounting to probable cause or not.[9]

In some areas of tort law, responsibility for making evaluative findings is divided between judge and jury, or other factfinder, but on a

[7] L.R. 3 H.L. 330 (1868).

[8] For example: Luthringer v. Moore, 31 Cal. 2d 489, 190 P.2d 1 (1948), holding that the question whether a case is a proper one for imposing strict liability is one of law for the court, and citing *Restatement, Torts,* § 520, comment h (1938): "What facts are necessary to make an activity ultrahazardous under the rule stated in this section is a matter for the judgment of the court." The same allocation of responsibility for the evaluative finding is carried forward in the tentative revision of the *Restatement of Torts,* though "abnormally dangerous" has replaced "ultrahazardous" in this formulation of strict liability. *Restatement (Second), Torts,* § 520 (Tent. Draft No. 10, 1964).

[9] For example, Stewart v. Sonneborn, 98 U.S. 187, 194 (1878) (dictum); *Restatement, Torts,* § 673(1)(c) (1938).

different basis from that applying to the issue of negligence. These are examples: (1) The evaluative finding of unreasonable interference with use and enjoyment of land that constitutes nuisance is sometimes left to a jury,[10] but in practice there has been considerably more judicial supervision in this area than in that of negligence. (2) The function of characterizing a communication as defamatory is divided between judge and jury, a common formulation being that the judge determines whether the communication is capable of a defamatory meaning, and the jury determines whether a defamatory meaning was conveyed.[11] (3) It has long been true that the function of making an evaluative finding that particular circumstances of publication give rise to a conditional privilege is assigned to the court, but the function of making an evaluative finding of abuse of the conditional privilege is assigned to the jury, with judicial supervision.[12] The supervision has become much more rigorous under *New York Times Co. v. Sullivan* [13] and *Time, Inc., v. Hill*,[14] but a division of responsibility between judge and jury continues.

In other areas, the allocation of responsibility is yet quite nebulous. These are examples: (1) the finding that an interference with one's interests amounts to an actionable invasion of privacy; [15] (2) the finding that conduct of the defendant inducing a third person to break a contract with plaintiff is tortious in quality; [16] (3) the finding that a product is "defective" in a sense supporting strict products liability.[17]

One of the current riddles of tort law, of pervasive significance, is whether any general principle is emerging concerning this problem of

[10] See *Restatement, Torts*, § 826 (1939). Comment d observes that the rules stated in §§ 829–831 have been developed for the guidance of trial courts and juries in weighing gravity against utility to determine whether an intentional invasion is unreasonable. Of course, the same kind of weighing of competing interests occurs in unintentional invasions alleged to amount to nuisance. See Prosser, *Torts* (3rd ed. 1964), § 88, p. 602.

[11] See, for example, Lane v. Washington Daily News, 85 F.2d 822, 824 (D.C. Cir. 1936) (dictum); Linehan v. Nelson, 197 N.Y. 482, 90 N.E. 1114 (1910); *Restatement, Torts*, § 614 (1938).

[12] For example, Hamilton v. Eno, 81 N.Y. 116 (1880); *Restatement, Torts*, § 619 (1938).

[13] 376 U.S. 254 (1964).

[14] 385 U.S. 374 (1967).

[15] See *Time, Inc., v. Hill*, 385 U.S. 374 (1967). Also see *Restatement, Torts*, § 867 (1939), and *Restatement (Second), Torts*, §§ 652A–652J (Tent. Draft No. 13, 1967), which are not explicit on this point.

[16] See *Restatement, Torts*, §§ 766–774 (1939), which are not explicit on this point.

[17] See below, Chapter 7.

allocating responsibility for evaluative findings as distinguished from findings of physical facts and events. It is a problem to which little direct attention is given. One aspect of its significance is its impact on the accommodation between creativity and continuity in the law. In general, predictability and consistency of decisions are reduced as the degree of judicial supervision of evaluative findings is reduced; not only opportunities for caprice and variation but also opportunities for trends of relatively unsupervised creativity are increased.

Perhaps there is warrant for the generalization that the trend of thought in modern tort law has favored greater dependence on doctrinal formulations requiring one-step application to particular cases and less dependence on formulations requiring two-step consideration of a prima facie theory of liability and privilege. The one-step method received its greatest boost in the nineteenth century development of negligence doctrine, which requires one-step weighing of risk against utility rather than second-step consideration of utility as a problem of privilege. Although it is not a logical compulsion that one-step formulations increase the role of the jury and decrease that of the court, in practice this appears to have been the result. Perhaps the determination that the issue of ultrahazardous or abnormally dangerous character of activity is one for the court presages a reversal of this trend. There remains a likelihood, however, that resort to a one-step formulation will result in submission to juries of evaluative problems that, if a two-step formulation had been used, might have been regarded as exclusively the province of judges, as second-step issues of privilege.

May this prove to be an incidental consequence of modification of the *Restatement* rule concerning severe mental distress?[18] The 1947 formulation of section 46 is in the two-step form of prima facie theory and privilege—"one who, without a privilege to do so, intentionally causes severe emotional distress" is subject to liability.[19] The amended formulation is in one-step form—"one who by extreme and outrageous conduct intentionally or recklessly causes severe emotional distress" is subject to liability.[20] Such a reformulation is more of a temptation to a

[18] I am indebted to my colleague Louis Jaffe for calling my attention to this apt illustration.

[19] *Restatement, Torts,* § 46 (Supp. 1948).

[20] *Restatement (Second), Torts,* § 46 (1965). Note particularly comment h: "*Court and jury.* It is for the court to determine, in the first instance, whether the defendant's conduct may reasonably be regarded as so extreme and outrageous as to permit recovery, or whether it is necessarily so. Where reasonable

73

troubled judge to leave the problem to the jury—taking their finding
on the outrageous quality of the conduct—than was the formulation
that separated the issue of privilege for independent consideration.

TRENDS OF JUDICIAL SUPERVISION

The most striking modern development bearing on the allocation of
responsibility between judge and jury in tort cases is the trend, notice-
able particularly in the post–World War II period, toward less judicial
supervision over jury findings of negligence. To some extent this trend
is reflected in modifications of verbal formulations, but to a greater extent it has been accomplished by a change in the meaning of formulations that have remained verbally constant or nearly so. Many cases
were allowed to go to a jury in the 1950's and thereafter on evidence
that in the 1930's would have been held insufficient to warrant reasoned inferences that the defendant was negligent and that the plaintiff was not. As a practical matter, in view of the obvious tendency of
juries in personal injury cases to resolve issues favorably to the plaintiff,
a significant reform in the prima facie basis of liability was accomplished in this way. Without doubt, the sense of need for such substantive reform in the law of torts was the most potent influence on the
development of this trend of less judicial supervision of verdicts.

Together with another tendency of juries—the tendency to reach
compromise verdicts when the evidence of contributory negligence is
rather persuasive, thereby fixing damages at a reduced figure and finding no contributory negligence—this development also accomplished a
significant movement toward apportioning damages in cases of contributory fault. Hardly anyone doubts the prevalence of this doctrinally
unlegitimated practice of jurors. Writing in 1961, Professor (later
Judge) Jack B. Weinstein, marshaling an array of empirical studies to
fortify the common judgment of trial lawyers about its prevalence,
argued that this practical rule of comparative negligence had become
so clearly a "substantive" part of the compensation system that it was
inappropriate for a United States district court, in the exercise of its
"procedural" control over diversity cases under the *Erie* doctrine, rou-
tinely to order the trial of damages issues separately from liability
issues.[21]

---

men may differ, it is for the jury, subject to the control of the court, to determine
whether, in the particular case, the conduct has been sufficiently extreme and
outrageous to result in liability."

[21] Weinstein, "Routine Bifurcation of Jury Negligence Trials: An Example
of the Questionable Use of Rule Making Power," 14 *Vand. L. Rev.* 831 (1961).

If one favors apportionment and keeps his eye on the resulting judgments only, he may take satisfaction in the existence of this rough form of comparative negligence, despite doctrinal adherence to the rule that contributory negligence is a complete bar. It has been urged that such doctrinally unlegitimated performance of the jury is an altogether laudable aspect of the legal system.[22] Certainly it is true that in some instances jury disregard for instructions—in some degree inevitable—has proved to be an aid to reform, in a manner somewhat analogous to the role of fictions in doctrinal development.[23] These benefits are to be accepted with grace. But their occasional occurrence is insufficient to justify a deliberate choice of this route as a means of law reform. And once disregard for instructions surpasses the bounds of occasional instances and becomes a pattern of common practice, courts and legislatures do the legal system a distinct disservice if they allow the general disregard to continue by nominally perpetuating the unsatisfactory doctrines that have produced it while practically countenancing the juries' application of a different rule. One can favor candid adoption of comparative negligence by legislation,[24] or even by judicial decision,[25] and yet find the adoption of that system by subterfuge deeply disturbing.

The creative role in the judicial system need not be limited to appellate courts. Trial judges should be free to act openly on the expressed belief that newly formulated qualifications and applications of doctrine are in keeping with the sense of pronouncements of the court of last resort, or even on the expressed belief that the court of last resort will overrule a well-established precedent when the occasion for reconsideration is presented.[26] But a distinction should be drawn be-

[22] Representative statements of position on this issue are collected in James, "Sufficiency of the Evidence and Jury-Control Devices Available before Verdict," 47 *Va. L. Rev.* 218, 247–248 (1961). James declares himself in favor of such a role for the jury in personal-injury litigation (p. 248, n. 146). Compare Harper and James, *Torts* (1956), vol. II, § 15.5, pp. 889–895. See also the dissenting opinion of Judge Sloan in Burghardt v. Olson, 354 P.2d 871, 876 (Ore. 1960), and the opposing view expressed in the specially concurring opinion of Judge O'Connell (at 875).

[23] There is a significant difference, however, between reform through doctrinal fictions and reform through juries' deviations from instructions. Beneficient doctrinal fictions are not intended to deceive. See Fuller, "Legal Fictions," 25 *Ill. L. Rev.* 363, 366–368 (1930). Thus, they may serve well the objectives of certainty and evenhandedness. The jury practice under discussion does not.

[24] See pp. 85–89 below.

[25] See pp. 45–53 above.

[26] See the dissenting opinion of Judge Woodbury in United States v. Girouard, 149 F.2d 760, 765 (1st Cir. 1945). And Judge Woodbury's prediction was soon proved correct. Girouard v. United States, 328 U.S. 61 (1946).

75

tween that kind of candidly creative action of a trial judge and the actions of trial judges and juries that effect change by regularly acting contrary to the authoritative pronouncements of the court of last resort.

The jury is not an appropriate body for a creative role in law reform. The claim that they are proficient in this role is based on their representation of community mores and attitudes. But the price in caprice and duplicity is too high for the advantage gained. The advantage should be assessed not in absolute terms of giving or denying force to community mores and attitudes, but rather in terms of the extent to which, if at all, juries are better suited for injecting this influence into the legal process than are appellate courts (or trial judges acting pursuant to their prediction of appellate court actions). No doubt there have been periods in our legal history, to one of which the Realist movement was a reaction, during which courts have been less sensitive to the views of society and to the needs for law reform than they should have been. But re-examination and revision of the creative role of judges, of the type occurring during the decade commencing in 1958, is a better solution to this problem than judicial acquiescence in the assumption of a creative role by juries, with the evils that inevitably follow.

The trend toward less and less supervision of evaluative findings by juries in negligence cases seems ill advised. It has been accepted, perhaps, with a sense of partial fulfillment of a need for reform, but accepted at a price that is too high. It is reform at the expense of integrity of the legal system and reform that is uneven in character, because judicial controls and supervision cannot be effectively exercised while the pretense is maintained that contributory negligence is a complete bar to recovery.

This is not to say, however, that we should restrict the range of cases in which juries are used in order to counteract this trend. Indeed, there are objections as grave, if not more so, to placing the power of ad hoc judgment in the hands of a professional adjudicator rather than the occasional adjudicators whose selection by chance for short periods of service and in groups gives a measure of protection against bias and corruption. The professional will not be content with an unorganized mass of ad hoc judgments, but will develop informally his own system of conceptual guides to decision if we deprive him of acknowledged doctrinal guides. Although such unexpressed guides produce a degree of consistency among the decisions of a single adjudicator, they offer no means of doing so on a broader scale.

We are too far away from an ultimate abdication of judicial supervision of evaluative jury findings to allow the specter at the end of the way to frighten us into blanket attacks on the jury system, but a view further down the road of generalized standards and unsupervised evaluative findings may serve to remind us that this is not the road of enlightened law reform. Rather it inevitably interjects a strong element of duplicity into those areas of the law, such as contributory negligence, in which legal doctrine is out of step with a well-developed community sense of what the law ought to be. In moving toward greater use of generalized standards in judicial doctrine as a route of reform, we have depended too much on the balm of duplicity to soothe the wounds of change, too little on the capacity of our legal system to absorb the shocks of candid creativity in the courts.

Historic jury trial has provided the advantages of a practical wisdom commonly found in a cross-section of the community and an extraordinary resistance to corruption and abuse of power. At the same time, it has assured evenhandedness through a measure of active supervision by judges. This sensitive balance is well worth maintaining.

Chapter 6
Drafting and Interpreting Statutes

$\mathcal{P}$ROTAGONISTS OF a more active role and greater freedom of technique for courts in private law reform have sometimes failed to recognize the need to revise, too, prevailing attitudes about the role and technique of legislatures. Remarks about the work of legislatures, casually inserted in discussions focused primarily on courts, often seem to be based on an assumption that, subject only to constitutional limitations, legislatures enjoy complete freedom in legislating. Closer examination of attitudes toward the legislative process reveals that the established tradition is actually far more restrictive. Indeed, we seem much nearer to exchanging rigid shackles for reasoned restraints in relation to processes of decisional reform than in relation to processes of statutory reform.

In both cases, some of the shackles have been forged from fiction. Judicial reform of decisional law was long restrained by the fiction that courts have no creative role of making law but only a ministerial role of finding and applying it. Statutory reform has been severely affected by an analogous fiction—that when courts interpret and apply statutes theirs is not a creative role but only the role of finding and applying the legislature's mandate. In what is perhaps its most extreme version, this fiction takes the form of a conclusive presumption that when a legislature undertakes to prescribe at all for a problem it prescribes in full.

This fiction can be expressed as a directive to courts. Thus formulated, it declares that when interpreting and applying a statute a court must proceed on the assumption that the legislature answered every question; the court's task is to find the legislature's answer and apply it.

In another form, addressed to a legislature, and especially to a legislative draftsman, this same theory says it is the legislature's task to answer every question. And the legislature is not supposed to depend on the court to exercise any creative role in fitting the statute into the body of cognate laws that are part of the setting in which the statute must operate.

We need not labor the point that these directives to courts and legislatures, though real, are unrealistic—that they are based on fiction. It is too plain for argument that neither a court in laying down a decisional doctrine nor a legislature in enacting a statute can possibly foresee and provide answers for all the questions that will arise. Thus, it is a matter not of choice but of necessity that courts act creatively when interpreting and applying statutes as well as when interpreting and applying decisional precedents.

Perhaps few judges and writers ever subscribe to this absolute presumption of complete prescription as a standard either for judicial interpretation or for legislative action. But it is hard to lay the ghost of this idea, for it rises up in subtler forms as courts, legislatures, and their critics consider problems of drafting and interpreting statutes.

REINTERPRETING STATUTES

Having once creatively interpreted a statute, what should a court do when it concludes in considering a subsequent case that its earlier interpretation was wrong—or, if you prefer to characterize it in some other way, unsound, unwise, unfair, injudicious, or unfaithful to the legislative mandate?

Can and should the court overrule its earlier interpretational decision, subject only to the same limitations it would apply in overruling one of its common law decisions? Not so, say many courts and writers. Here we encounter a restrictive view that the court must or should treat its own interpretation as partaking of the same quality as the statutory text itself, commanding a special respect and having a special immunity from revision by the court. Why?

The fiction of complete prescription is a ready answer often relied upon in some degree at least. The legal rule previously declared by the court was found in the statute, it is said, and that rule can be changed only by the legislature.

This is not to say that the fiction of complete prescription is the only answer given. Indeed there are arguments of substance that deserve close examination. "Ordinarily," it has been asserted, "a principle to be great enough to justify a reversal of legislative interpretation must be a matter for the Constitution." Partly the reasons advanced are concerned with pressures exerted upon lawmakers. If courts are free "to reinterpret legislation, the result will be to relieve the legislature from pressure." And courts will be likely to act indecisively in the face of pressure, doing "enough to prevent legislative revision and not much

79

more." [1] One is reminded of arguments against prospective overruling on the ground that it relieves the pressure on courts to overrule retroactively, leading them to adopt measures of reform that are less decisive and, by the critics' standards, less worthy.[2] In both cases, however, it may sometimes be that the principal need can be met by a less drastic measure.

It is true that the greater flexibility of process achieved by recognizing an additional method as a legitimate technique of reform serves to reduce the pressure for using a more rigorous or far-reaching method of reform. But it sometimes happens also that, first, this is meeting the principal need for reform in the least disturbing way, and, second, reform can be achieved in this way long before it would be possible to muster the support necessary for a more drastic measure of reform.

Perhaps the most suggestive and cogent of the ideas advanced in support of the restrictive point of view about reinterpreting statutes is that "the democratic process seems to require that controversial changes should be made by the legislative body." [3] Beyond doubt there is a difference between courts and legislatures with respect to their fitness for making controversial changes. But the restrictive conclusion urged does not follow from logical necessity, and the adverse practical impact it would have is a weighty consideration against it. Indeed, the doctrine that a court should never overrule its own interpretations of a statute, except on constitutional grounds, would effect a more severe restriction upon the creative work of courts than any doctrine ever applied either to common law precedents or to initial interpretation of statutes.

INTERPRETING STATUTES IN CASES OF FIRST IMPRESSION

Restraints on judicial reinterpretation of statutes, though perhaps the most dramatic of the restrictions on the court's work of interpreting and applying statutes, are not the most significant. Rather, they merely add to the impact of restrictive concepts applied in the more numerous cases of interpretation that are seen as distinguishable from others previously decided and therefore as cases of first impression.

If a court is imbued with the idea that the legislature is supposed to prescribe fully and the court is supposed to respect the legislature's ac-

[1] Levi, "An Introduction to Legal Reasoning," 15 *U. Chi. L. Rev.* 501, 540 (1948).
[2] See above, p. 41.
[3] Levi, "An Introduction to Legal Reasoning," p. 523.

tion, then it is likely to presume, as suggested before, that the legislature has answered all the questions. The court's task then is simply to discover in the statute and its context what those prescribed answers are. Since the answers are not plainly written on the face of the statute, the court must have some technique other than merely reading the statute to find them. The technique commonly resorted to is to find an intent or purpose from which answers can be deduced. This general idea has been dressed in various garbs.

One of them, surely predominant for a time and invoked frequently if not usually even today, is that the court must seek out and apply the intent of the legislature when answering questions confronted in applying a statute. This theory is extended particularly to those difficult questions as to which the statute plainly does not express an answer, with the consequence that the court is inferring a legislature's intent from whatever sources it regards as legitimate evidence of that intent.

It has long been recognized, of course, that it is fiction to speak of the intent of either the individual legislator or the legislative body. For this reason, some have preferred to speak of the intent or purpose of the legislation rather than the intent or purpose of the legislature or individual legislators. This way of speaking suggests that there is an internal logic in the statute. Even though the statute itself has not spelled out all the corollaries and implications, if one can discover that internal logic he can expand upon it through reasoned inferences and thereby reach answers to questions not dealt with explicitly. This theory provides a useful approach to interpretation when the internal logic of the statute is sufficiently developed to support a framework of reason for answering the question at issue. But often this is not the case. Just as surely as the legislature fails to answer explicitly all the questions that may arise in applying a statute, so too it fails to provide manifestations of a complete internal logic from which the answers can be derived by inference.

Hart and Sacks have contributed a significant improvement upon this idea of an internal system of order embedded in the statute by the legislature. Rather than describing the process of interpretation as a search for the purpose of the legislature or even the purpose of the statute as an existing datum, they refer to the process as one of "attribution of purpose."[4] The court is thus asking itself what purpose it attributes to the statute. This way of putting the question opens up a

[4] Hart and Sacks, *The Legal Process,* pp. 1413–1417.

wide range of inquiry about how the statute can best be interpreted and applied so it is correlated with the total body of cognate laws to produce evenhanded justice. This helps to avoid bizarre discriminations that the language of the statute might seem to support but that no one could suppose a legislature would have enacted if the question had been placed before them explicitly.

I do not understand Hart and Sacks to imply that the purpose to be attributed to the statute need be one that was or even could have been consciously formulated at the time the statute was enacted. I understand them to choose this formulation for the very reason that they wish to free the court from the handicaps of dealing in the fiction that the statute contains within it an answer to every question that might arise in its application. But can we be confident that persons using their formulation would not lapse into that fiction and think of the purpose of the statute rather than the purpose attributed to it? I fear that many of the judges, lawyers, and writers using the Hart and Sacks formulation would still tend to act and think as if they were, when "attributing" a purpose, getting answers out of the statute rather than creatively formulating answers themselves. This is especially likely because of the natural uneasiness of a judge and his critics about whether he is playing false to his obligation to respect the policy decisions of the legislature when he attributes purpose rather than finding it.

Let us face squarely an important aspect of the scope of the judge's obligation to respect the legislative mandate. Surely there is full agreement that if the statute contains evidence that the legislature has considered a question and prescribed an answer to it, the court must respect and apply that answer, subject to constitutional limitations on the legislature's action and subject perhaps to other rarely applicable qualifications such as the doctrine of desuetude. The difficulty and doubt arise only when it is not clear that the legislature has considered and answered a question, or when it is clear that it has not; in these circumstances, the court's task is inevitably creative.

A court's refusal to acknowledge its inevitably creative role in statutory interpretation is unrealistic and crippling even in the disposition of a single case. From a long range point of view, such refusal freezes reform. When legislatures intrude into an area of private law, the court considers itself no longer free either to overrule or to innovate interstitially. In view of the ever increasing impact of inertia in legislatures, the effect in most cases is a deep freeze.

The restrictive impact of the fiction that a statute does or should provide either a complete set of answers, or a manifestation of purpose from which a complete set of answers can be inferred, is the more severe because it affects not only the working attitudes of courts but also the working attitudes of legislatures. They, too, may be persuaded that they are powerless to provide, at the time of first legislating, against the deep-freeze effect that courts have been wont to read into statutory enactments.

Suppose that a legislature wishes to effect a needed reform in private law regarding any of several live issues—for example, whether to adopt comparative negligence in lieu of the rule that contributory negligence is a complete bar, or whether to allow contribution among tortfeasors. Suppose also that the legislature wishes neither to assume responsibility for the continuing supervision of the area of law affected nor to withdraw from the courts the power of supervision they exercise in the absence of intrusion by the legislature. Is there no way for a legislature to accomplish such an objective? The deep-freeze view would seem to answer that question in the negative. The legislature is thus confronted with the hard choice between the extremes of doing nothing and assuming almost exclusive responsibility for continuing supervision of the area of law.

Even worse, under this view a legislature's assumption of responsibility is nigh irreversible. How would the legislature withdraw, assuming it wished to do so? If it merely repealed the statute enacted, would that not restore the law that existed before the statute was enacted? Worse still, would it not restore it with an imprimatur of the legislature—an imprimatur that the courts, by the deep-freeze view, would be required to respect? If the legislature had never spoken in the first instance, the courts would have had some power, at the least, to overrule their own doctrine.

If this view were to prevail, over the course of time there would be an ever increasing responsibility upon the legislature for reform of private law, and an ever diminishing control of the courts over outmoded law. And while this was occurring, legislatures would be growing less and less capable of exercising the more extensive responsibility because of their preoccupation with matters more clearly political.

Perhaps the most significant missing ingredient in this view of legislation is some theory under which legislatures can venture into an area of private law for the purpose of effecting a needed change without thereby accomplishing, as an undesired by-product, a permanent assumption of wider responsibility—and correlatively a permanent destruction of the power of courts to develop legal doctrine that is well designed to do justice.

Of course it will be argued that any deviation from the restrictive path of the deep-freeze tradition is unconstitutional—that it impinges upon the constitutional separation of powers between courts and legislatures. In response, let it be clear that what is proposed here is not a complete leveling that would destroy the distinction between the roles of legislatures and courts in dealing with private law reform. Rather, the proposal is to make a far more modest change in thinking about these roles. In terms of broad principle, the question might be put in this way: In relation to private law reform, has our tradition defined ideally the role that each of these two institutions, legislatures and courts, is best able to fulfill? Or might a thorough re-examination produce a somewhat different allocation of responsibilities and powers from that implied in our current legal tradition?

DELEGATING SUPERVISION OVER LAW REVISION

When we examine closely the performance of legislatures, we find that in fact some techniques are in common use for delegating to other bodies—courts, administrative agencies, and even juries—a considerable measure of power and responsibility for law reform. It would be error to accept as a valid statement of our legal tradition that the legislature must assume exclusive responsibility for the future reform of any area of private law in which it undertakes to enact legislation.

The necessity that a court act creatively when interpreting and applying statutes is also, when seen in another light, a necessity that the legislature leave to the court some role in making law even in those areas into which the legislature intrudes by enacting statutes. The legislature has great latitude, however, to determine the scope of the role a particular enactment leaves to courts (and to other agencies as well, including administrative agencies and juries). This is a power it necessarily exercises coincidentally if not deliberately. There is nothing improper about exercising the power deliberately.

One way in which this power is exercised is through the degree of specificity of statutory mandates. In creating new doctrine, legislatures, like courts, must face a choice between generalized and particularized doctrines. Particularized doctrines leave to other agencies relatively little leeway. Generalized doctrines, on the other hand, leave broad scope for law reform by other agencies. For example, compare statutes prescribing rules of the road for motorists with antitrust statutes. The former are rather particularized; the latter, so general in character that their practical impact depends very greatly on interpretations by courts and enforcement policies of executive or administrative agencies. Perhaps there is implicit a possibility for participation even by juries, though in practice their participation has not been as significant in the antitrust area as in some others.

One example will serve to illustrate both the fact of jury discretion and the fact that even the more particularized legislation does not preclude the exercise of some discretion by juries, as well as other agencies. The example is the performance of juries, whether by design or not, in determining effective rules of law concerning contributory fault as a bar in personal injury actions arising from traffic accidents. Statutory rules of the road for motorists have not served to preclude jury participation in lawmaking in this way. This is a fact we must recognize, whether in praise or in criticism.

An example of a different kind of solution with respect to generality and particularity of statutory standards is the income tax law, which specifies considerable detail in the statute itself, but leaves still further detail to be developed by an administrative agency and by courts.

Despite the necessity that the legislature leave to the courts part of the creative task of elaborating details of a new statutory scheme of law, and despite the practice of legislatures in commonly delegating to courts and to other agencies, through somewhat generalized mandates, a far greater creative role than necessity demands, still our legal tradition seems bent on concealing rather than openly facing these facts and the problems of legal process implicit in them. To what extent should a legislature, when reforming an area of substantive law, do so in a way that preserves judicial responsibility for future development of that area—including future reform? Perhaps it seems a break with tradition even to ask this question. Yet every time a legislature enacts a statue it gives an implicit answer by necessity, if it does not consider and answer the question deliberately. Is it not better to face the question squarely?

Consider the doctrine that contributory negligence bars a claim for damages based on negligence. A consensus for reform of this doctrine, slowly building for a long time, appears to be gaining momentum. The old rule is compatible neither with the principle of basing awards for accidental injuries on fault nor with newer principles of strict liability or insurance. Barring all recovery because of contributory negligence deviates from the proposition that losses should be allocated according to fault. It produces instead the bizarre result that when one driver in a two-car collision is grievously negligent and slightly injured and the other slightly negligent and grievously injured, the person slightly negligent suffers grievous loss and the person grievously negligent suffers slight loss.

Hardly anyone has ever doubted the competence of a legislature to enact a comparative negligence statute. And few, if any, would doubt the competence of a court to adopt a comparative negligence system initially, when considering the issue as genuinely one of first impression. But restrictive views of the competence of courts to overrule their own decisions have stood in the way of judicial adoption of comparative negligence in jurisdictions having precedents or an understood tradition supporting the contributory fault rule.

In Chapter 3 it has been suggested that this traditional view should no longer prevail—that a state court of last resort should consider itself competent to adopt a system of comparative negligence and responsible for facing that substantive issue on the merits rather than declining on grounds of stare decisis even to consider whether the rule is so bad that overruling is appropriate. At this point, in contrast, the question posed is whether a legislature has any choice between the one extreme of designing and enacting a complete comparative negligence system and the other of taking no action. Must the legislature do all or nothing?

The comparative negligence problem is not one of extraordinary difficulty, but it cannot be solved completely with a few well chosen statutory phrases. As we have already seen, one who is designing a complete system of comparative negligence must decide, among other things: (1) whether to make it a pure system (apportioning damages in all cases of contributory negligence, even when the plaintiff was more negligent than defendant) or a limited system (the most common limitation being that apportionment applies only when the plaintiff was less negligent than the defendant); (2) whether to use special interrogatories to juries in aid of judicial control over comparative negligence findings by juries; (3) whether to provide that liability insurance covers only the liability of an insured after an offset because of his own losses or instead covers percentages of loss proportioned to fault without offset.

To illustrate this last question, suppose A and B, equally negligent in operating their respective cars, collide with each other, causing $500 damage to A's vehicle and $600 to B's. Assume also that the first of the three questions above is answered in favor of a pure form of apportionment. Will the result then be that A's liability insurer pays $50 (one half of A's net liability of $100) and B's liability insurer pays nothing, or instead that they pay respectively $300 (one half of B's damage of $600) and $250 (one half of A's damage of $500)? Must a legislature answer this question in order for its attempt at enacting a comparative negligence statute to be valid and effective? It would seem not. At least, this view is implicit in what legislatures and courts have done in the states having comparative negligence statutes. Customarily these statutes give no explicit answer to the problem of offsets when liability insurance is involved. Nor do they provide the answer by any manifestation of purpose express or implied. Despite this omission these statutes are regularly enforced without even a suggestion that their validity is in question on this account.

Suppose that a majority of the legislature desire a change to comparative negligence but consider that the supreme court of the state is a better forum in which to develop all the details of the system than is the legislature. What might the legislature do?

A statute on comparative negligence might contain a core sentence as follows: "Contributory negligence shall not be a complete bar to recovery of damages by a person suffering accidental injuries."

If the legislature says nothing more than this, should a court say that the legislative attempt is inoperative—for example, because it is void for vagueness, or because it is an attempt to delegate legislative power to courts in contravention of the constitutional separation of powers?

This one sentence states an essential difference—perhaps the most essential difference—between the common law doctrine that contributory fault is a complete bar and the comparative negligence doctrine that contributory fault may be taken into account to reduce damages but not to bar completely. It nevertheless leaves a host of questions undecided. Among them is the question whether a "pure" or a "limited" form of comparative negligence is to be applied. That is, will apportionment apply even when the plaintiff is more negligent than the defendant or only when the defendant is more negligent than the plaintiff? Who is to decide that question? Is it possible for a legislature to delegate that power of decision to the courts?

May it be that the question is improperly phrased when stated in terms of delegation since "delegation" implies that it is the legislature's responsibility that is being discharged, even if the task is being done by the court? Should we ask instead: Is it proper for a legislature to enact a mandate declaring some change in a common law doctrine created initially by the courts, while leaving to the courts most of the responsibility for remaking their own doctrine in a way that will mesh reasonably and fairly with the new legislative mandate?

Consider an alternative to this core statutory sentence that exposes another problem of choice of expression somewhat analogous to that regarding "delegation." Suppose a sentence as follows: "The doctrine that contributory negligence is a complete bar to recovery for accidentally inflicted injuries is hereby abrogated."

Is "abrogated" the right word, or at least a satisfactory word, to convey the meaning intended? Would it be appropriate to say "repealed"? A legislature repeals legislation, but does it repeal judicially created doctrine? Would it be appropriate to say "overruled"? A court overrules doctrine, but does a legislature overrule? Is the difference deeper than linguistic custom? If not, perhaps we can avoid the argument by just saying "abrogated." Assume that we have found a way of answering or avoiding that question—by using "abrogated" or by using the first form of sentence rather than the alternative.

Consider, now, the possibility that the legislature, whether compelled to do so or not, wishes to say more though still without purporting to answer all questions. The following proposals for additions to the core sentence disclose a wide range of degrees of specificity a legislature might consider.

First: "The formulation of details of a new doctrine to replace that abrogated is hereby explicitly committed to the courts of this state."

Does this sentence say anything more than is necessarily implied if the legislature enacts only the core sentence? Is it inappropriate for the legislature to be explicit in this way?

When other explicit additions to the core sentence are being included in a comparative negligence statute, an alternative way of expressing the idea of this first addition might be used. That is, other additional provisions might be preceded by an introductory phrase such as "Under rules to be formulated by the courts of this state . . ."

Second: "In cases of contributory negligence, damages recoverable shall be fairly and equitably proportionate to fault."

One might argue that this, too, says nothing that is not necessarily implied in the core sentence. He would be met by an argument that this sentence, stating a standard and omitting any requirement that the plaintiff be less negligent than the defendant, lends support to a judicial interpretation of the statute as adopting the pure rather than the limited form of comparative negligence. If the legislative draftsman adverted to the problem and wished to answer it in this way, he would be more likely to add to his draft in a way such as that suggested next.

Third: "Contributory negligence shall be a basis for fairly and equitably reducing rather than barring recovery, regardless of whether the person seeking recovery was less at fault than the one against whom recovery is sought."

These three suggestions are merely illustrative. One who gives his imagination free rein can think of other provisions expressing in various degrees, ranging from the most general to the most particular, guidelines for decision of particular cases.

A like range of choice would be confronted in drafting statutes on other substantive issues. As another example, consider contribution among tortfeasors. A core sentence might read: "The rule against contribution among tortfeasors is hereby abrogated." This might be followed by a variety of other provisions.

First: "The formulation of details of a new doctrine to replace that abrogated is hereby explicitly committed to the courts of this state."

Second: "Except insofar as he is held liable for intentional wrongdoing, a tortfeasor shall be permitted to recover fair and equitable contribution from others who are subject to liability for the same harm for which he is liable." The sentence might stop here, or it might answer another question by continuing, "and this rule shall apply to payments made in settlement as well as payments made upon judgments."

Consider another possibility. Why not simply adopt by statute a precedent from another state?[5] For example, in the area of contribu-

[5] Compare a suggestion made in the "Report of the Committee on the Establishment of a Permanent Organization for the Improvement of the Law Proposing the Establishment of an American Law Institute." "If the principles of law set forth in the restatement are not to be adopted as a formal code it is nevertheless not impossible that they may be adopted by state legislatures with

tion among tortfeasors the United States Court of Appeals for the District of Columbia, in a carefully considered opinion in the case of *Knell v. Feltman*,[6] adopted for that jurisdiction a rule of contribution among tortfeasors. Might a statute be drafted to adopt that precedent? Consider this formulation: "The doctrine disallowing contribution among tortfeasors is hereby abrogated. The opinion in the case of *Knell v. Feltman*, 174 F.2d 662 (D.C. Cir. 1949), is hereby adopted for this state as if a decision of the supreme court of this state."

Or, suppose that in the enacting state there is a particular precedent that the legislature disapproves, as was the case in New York after the Court of Appeals had decided against allowing legal relief to an attractive young lady who sued because the defendant, without her consent, adorned its flour sacks with her photograph, adding the inscription "Flour of the Family." [7] The core sentence of the responsive statute might read as follows: "The decision of the Court of Appeals of this state in the case of *Roberson v. Rochester Folding Box Company* is hereby disapproved." [8]

For a continuation of the statute, if the legislature must add more for valid legislation or chooses to do so even if it need not, these are some of the possibilities. First: "An actionable right of privacy shall be recognized in like cases in the future." Second: "An actionable right of privacy shall be recognized in like cases in the future, and in other cases in which the courts of this state deem it appropriate to allow an action in light of the actions here declared to be allowable."

The legislature might, instead, take a different course. Consider some further examples. Third: "When the issue is hereafter presented in the courts of this state in causes of action based on incidents occurring on

---

the proviso that they shall have the force of principles enunciated as the basis of the decisions of the highest court of the state, the courts having power to declare modifications and exceptions." 1 *ALI Proceedings* 24 (1923).

[6] 174 F.2d 662 (D.C. Cir. 1949). Included in the opinion was the following passage. "We conclude that when a tort is committed by the concurrent negligence of two or more persons who are not intentional wrongdoers, contribution should be enforced; that a joint judgment against such tort-feasors is not a prerequisite to contribution between them, and it is immaterial whether they were, or any of them was, personally negligent." The court also quotes with approval an earlier decision to this effect: "[W]hen the parties are not intentional and willful wrongdoers, but are made so by legal inference or intendment, contribution may be enforced."

[7] Roberson v. Rochester Folding Box Co., 171 N.Y. 538, 64 N.E. 442 (1902).

[8] For a like proposal and additional suggestions presented in problem form, together with relevant materials, see Hart and Sacks, *The Legal Process*, pp. 798–817.

or after the effective date of this statute, the courts shall treat it as an issue of first impression." Fourth: "The decision of the Supreme Court of the State of Georgia in *Pavesich v. New England Life Insurance Co.,* 122 Ga. 190, 50 S.E. 68 (1905), recognizing a legally enforceable right of privacy, is hereby adopted for this state as if it had been rendered by the highest court of this state."

Even assuming that all these formulations are appropriate as methods of legislation—and this has not been asserted—one still would very likely draw the line short of the following. Fifth: "The views expressed in Warren and Brandeis, 'The Right to Privacy,' 4 *Harvard Law Review* 193 (1890), are hereby adopted as the law of this state."

Techniques of legislation regarded as appropriate in some contexts would not be appropriate for every type of legislative problem. Thus, the very simple statutes of the type suggested seem far easier to support and defend for the areas of contribution among tortfeasors and the contributory fault rule than for other areas of the law that come readily to mind.

As one example, consider the need for reform in automobile tort and insurance law. The Basic Protection plan for compensating traffic victims is founded on two principles: to reimburse net losses regardless of fault up to a moderate limit, through insurance; and to eliminate most claims based on negligence except when the injuries are quite severe.[9] Would it be appropriate to adopt a statute simply enacting this statement of principles as part of the law of the state? Even without a careful analysis of the problem, it is apparent that it would be much more difficult to justify this kind of statute than to justify one of the kinds suggested above in relation to contributory fault and contribution among tortfeasors.

As one approach to the question whether a legislature should be permitted to legislate in ways like those illustrated above (excluding the examples of adopting by reference views expressed elsewhere and enacting merely a statement of two underlying principles for reforming automobile accident law), compare what they would be doing with what in fact they have done traditionally. It is common that statutes are incomplete in a manner analogous to the treatment—or nontreatment—by comparative negligence statutes of the problem of offset in liability insurance situations. Examples abound, too, of statutes prescribing only in very general terms. Occasionally a statute names the

[9] See below, Chapter 8.

target case explicitly in abrogating a precedent and prescribing in very general terms. Hart and Sacks have called attention, among other instructive examples, to "declaratory legislation" directing that a pre-existing judicial decision shall not be "deemed" or "construed" to have a stated meaning.[10] Thus legislatures do in fact act in ways that implicitly commit to courts responsibility for filling out details consistently with a rather generalized legislative mandate.

Perhaps it is relevant, too, that legislatures as institutions and legislators individually do in fact leave much to the discretion of others even when formulating relatively detailed statutory prescriptions. What happens in a legislature when a bill on contribution among tortfeasors comes before it? To what extent do legislators vote on principles and to what extent upon all the details of the statutory draft? If they rely upon fellow legislators, or staff personnel, or advisers outside the legislature, perhaps even including law professors, is the problem of "delegation" sharply different from what it would be if they "delegated" the development of details to the courts of the state?

One may answer that there is a difference in that the job of formulation is done for them before their final vote, rather than after. A difference there surely is, but whether it should be critical is another matter. On this point it is relevant that the legislature does not lose control by enacting a generalized statute. It still has the power to modify anything the supreme court of the state thereafter does. This it can do by enacting subsequent legislation.

POLITICAL ISSUES IN PRIVATE LAW REFORM

Though both courts and legislatures are lawmaking institutions, their capabilities and legitimate roles differ. One important difference is that legislatures are free to adopt measures of law reform regardless of the degree to which they affect or become involved in current political controversy, but courts quite appropriately abstain from initiating reforms that, in the context, would be generally regarded as essentially political in nature.

---

[10] Hart and Sacks, *The Legal Process*, pp. 805–807. One of the examples to which they call attention, constitutional rather than statutory, is the Eleventh Amendment to the Constitution of the United States: "The Judicial power of the United States shall not be construed to extend to any suit in law or equity, commenced or prosecuted against one of the United States by Citizens of another State, or by Citizens or Subjects of any Foreign State." It was adopted in protest against the Supreme Court's decision in Chisholm v. Georgia, 2 U.S. (2 Dall.) 419 (1793). "What the Court has, in effect, done is to treat the Eleventh Amendment as if it were a precedent to the opposite of Chisholm v. Georgia" (Hart and Sacks, p. 807).

Thus, for example, courts do not ordinarily modify civil rights law—such as rules concerning fair housing, voting rights, and intrusions upon property for civil rights protests—except on constitutional grounds. Modifications other than those grounded in a constitution are left to legislatures as political questions. But rights to damages under some segment of tort law may be treated very differently. For example, although doctrines concerning the wife's right to an action for loss of consortium in consequence of an injury to her husband may get involved in politics, the question is not political in a sense requiring that courts refrain from dealing with it on their own in the absence of action by the legislature.

The classification of a question as "nonpolitical" in the sense described here does not mean that the legislature is unable to act in that area or even that it has any obligation to defer to the courts. It does mean, however, that the legislature may depend more upon the courts than it may in relation to political issues. Its power over and responsibility for the law concerning the nonpolitical problem is, if it wishes, shared with courts in far greater degree than is possible in relation to problems that are essentially political.

Associated with the distinction between the legislature's freedom to engage in essentially political action and the court's obligation to act nonpolitically is a difference with respect to the freedom of judges and legislators to participate in public debate. In general, a legislator is free to speak publicly or privately, anytime and anywhere, about his own views as to what should be done by the legislature of which he is a member when some issue of private law reform comes before it. On the other hand, tradition has it—and wisely so it would seem—that the members of a court are not free to make speeches or write law review articles urging that an issue expected to come before their court should be resolved in a certain way.

The distinction connoted by referring to issues as political or nonpolitical in this sense is not one that has been or is likely to be formulated with precision. But it would seem clear, at least, that something rather precise can be said in the negative. That is, it is error to assert or assume, as is sometimes done, that a legislature's choosing to act upon a problem of private law reform makes that problem political in this sense. Rather, such limitations as there are upon potential judicial action merely because of the legislature's action are due to the courts' obligation to respect the legislative mandate. Thus, courts continue to have both competence and responsibility for lawmaking insofar as the legislative mandate is incomplete. This is a corollary of the proposition that a legislature need not deprive a court of its continuing responsibility for supervising and developing the law on all aspects of the problem other than those for which the legislature prescribes. It need not, when enacting a private law reform, convert the whole private law problem into one essentially political in nature in a sense that precludes future modification by judicial action. It is free to decline such near exclusive future responsibility for an area of law into which it has intruded.

SOME TENTATIVE GUIDELINES

As a framework for guidelines courts might use in interpreting statutes, and guidelines legislatures might use in devising statutes that must be interpreted by courts, four propositions are suggested. They are stated here in a form addressed to a judge facing a problem of interpreting and applying a statute. They might be characterized as obligations of fidelity to the legislature's mandate, deference to the legislature's manifestations of principle and policy, creative adaptation to the manifested principles and policies, and candid appraisal of the scope of both the mandate and the manifestations of principle and policy.

First: Apply the mandate of the statute if it appears that the legislature did in fact both consider and prescribe for the problem at hand.

Second: If the problem falls beyond the core area that the legislature both considered and prescribed for, defer to the legislature's manifested determinations of principle and policy to the extent they can be ascertained and are relevant to the problem at hand.[11]

Third: Subject to the obligations to apply the legislature's mandate and defer to its manifestations of principle and policy, resolve the problem at hand in a way that in the court's view produces the best total set of rules, including those within the core area of the statute and other cognate rules of law, whatever their source.

Fourth: In deciding the scope of both the legislature's mandate and its manifestations of principle and policy, appraise the available evidence candidly and without resort to any contrary-to-fact presump-

[11] Compare the opinion of the court, delivered by Frankfurter, J., in Universal Camera Corp. v. NLRB, 340 U.S. 474, 487 (1951): "It is fair to say that in all this Congress expressed a mood. And it expressed its mood not merely by oratory but by legislation. As legislation that mood must be respected, even though it can only serve as a standard for judgment and not as a body of rigid rules assuring sameness of application."

tions; employ a rebuttable presumption that the legislature is ordinarily clear about its considered mandates, leaving courts to act in accordance with the second and third guidelines with respect to questions it does not clearly answer.

These four guidelines represent only a way of approaching statutory interpretation. They are not intended as a set of canons of construction that operate with logical precision to dictate an answer. Indeed, experience with canons purporting to serve with such precision suggests that they may do more harm than good. But that does not mean that guidelines as general as these would have no practical impact. Even as brief and general as they are, these guidelines contradict the fiction of complete prescription. Accepting them would help to avoid the disabling deep freeze that the fiction tends to sustain. Perhaps there is little danger that the fiction will be accepted in its most brazen form, even without the benefit of such guidelines as these. But experience suggests that subtler forms of the fiction continue even today to plague the whole process of legislating and interpreting legislation.

These guidelines, it is submitted, represent a candid statement of what courts in fact often do when they succeed in escaping fully from the fiction of complete prescription.

Guidelines are needed also with respect to when it is appropriate for a legislature to use deliberately a very generalized form of statute—one that leaves to courts a relatively large measure of responsibility for continued development and redevelopment of the details of the legal doctrine initiated by the statute. The following are offered as the beginning, at least, of such a set of guidelines.

First: It is within a legislature's competence to wipe the slate clean of a judicial precedent regarded as undesirable, leaving the court as much freedom thereafter as if it were facing an issue on which there had never been any precedent in the jurisdiction.

Second: With respect to substantive issues as to which a court would be competent to overrule its own precedents, a legislature is competent to change the law in a way that preserves for the state's court of last resort as much freedom as it would have had after it had overruled its own precedent.

Before courts began to make use of the technique of prospective overruling, it might have been said that overruling decisions were always particularized in one sense at least—they decided the case sub judice. But their impact as precedent is far greater in relation to cases not precisely like the one decided. Thus it is common for precedents to be described by a statement of principle. For example, *MacPherson v. Buick Motor Company* [12] stands for the proposition that in general lack of privity is no defense for a manufacturer who negligently places on the market a product that causes injury. The qualifying phrase "in general" is essential to the accuracy of this statement because Cardozo's opinion in that case was thoroughly hedged about with cautionary signals that the precise scope of the change was not then determined. Incidentally, that was an opinion, also, that did not openly overrule precedents but purported to formulate a principle implicit in the precedents though not previously expressed. But let us treat the case as history has treated it, as a decision making new law. If a court can make a change as inconclusive and indeterminate as this, should not a legislature be free to direct a change in a similarly generalized way, likewise leaving the development of details to judicial decisions in future cases? To deny that power is to sharply limit the legislature's powers over outmoded decisional doctrine, for it is so much more difficult and time-consuming to prescribe in detail that legislatures rarely find it feasible to do so.

Third: It is within a legislature's competence to prescribe somewhat more precisely without undertaking to prescribe in full detail.

Fourth: It is within a legislature's competence to retreat from its own detailed prescription to a more generalized prescription—one that leaves more to the courts. It makes no sense, on any policy ground, to hold that a legislature's decision to prescribe a detailed reform of some area of decisional law is irreversible in perpetuity. Indeed, perhaps a case can be made for the proposition that prescription in perpetuity ought to be forbidden. But for the present, let us stand on only the former, more modest proposition. A corollary is that a legislature should have the power to repeal its detailed statute and restore to the courts the power and responsibility for continued development of the area of law in question to the same degree as if the legislature had never prescribed in detail. Similarly, it should be able to repeal a detailed prescription and lay down instead a generalized mandate that would leave the courts not as free as if no legislative mandate had been given, but free to develop details differently from the way the legislature had done in its first effort.

In referring to issues concerning which courts are competent to act,

[12] 217 N.Y. 382, 111 N.E. 1050 (1916).

these guidelines take account of the fact, already noted, that some problems are so political in nature that the competence of courts to deal with them is sharply restricted. A corollary is that in respect to such problems legislatures have less freedom to depend on courts to keep the law responsive to current needs.

Legislative mandates of the more generalized among the kinds permitted under these guidelines have been rarely used in practice. But this need not be taken as evidence that such generalized prescriptions are regarded as beyond the competence of legislatures. Rather, this circumstance may result from the choice not to exercise the power. The correct explanation of the rarity of exercise of the legislative power to prescribe in relatively general rather than particular terms may be concerned more with practicalities of the legislative process than with restrictive views of the freedom of the legislature to choose between generalized and particularized statutory drafting. When questions are raised during legislative hearings or debate, fears can be calmed and assurances can be given far more effectively with statutory language than with the assertion that the courts will reasonably apply the generalized mandate of the statute.

In some circumstances, however, specificity in statutory prescription might make it impossible to get the necessary accumulation of votes from partisans of different interests, each hoping that the general statutory language can be developed in its favor as the process of interpretation and application by the courts advances.

Practicalities of the legislative process will influence the degree of specificity of statutes perhaps even more than principles concerned with wisely allocating responsibilities among courts and legislatures for continuing supervision over the revision of private law. But that is not to say that legislatures will ignore these considerations. Thus, the more clearly they can be elucidated, and the more generally they can be accepted and supported, the more effect they will have in influencing legislatures, as well as courts, to perform their law reform functions in ways designed to maintain over the long span of time the capacity of the legal system to renew itself.

Two

Two Areas of Major Substantive Change

Chapter 7

Harms from Products and Services

*P*ROCESSES of private law reform and the substantive issues they treat are interwoven into a single fabric of controversy. The point is well illustrated in the struggle to modernize the law of products liability. This is the law applying to a claim that personal injury or property damage has been caused by some characteristic of a product for which one or more of those in the chain of production and marketing should be held legally responsible.

When focusing primarily on changes in substantive principles of products liability, we could not, if we wished, escape recurring overtones of controversy over processes. We can, if we will, better understand the substantive controversy by returning, at least occasionally, to an examination of the processes by which substantive change may be achieved. As we shall see in the latter part of this chapter, for example, a major controversy over the applicability of the provisions of the Uniform Commercial Code concerning disclaimers turns out to be at least as much a controversy over the judiciary's role in interpreting statutes as over substantive legal principles.

THE ERA OF STRICT PRODUCTS LIABILITY

Arrival of the era of strict products liability was no longer in doubt after the year 1963. Decisions advancing this principle since 1963 have been described as a tidal wave, a flood, and a prairie fire—expressions that disclose varied geographical points of view but perhaps a common ideological perspective of foreboding. Others, whose comments speak of the same development but from a different ideological perspective, hail a breakthrough, a new insight, and (as I have just stated, thus revealing my bias) a new era.

These striking changes in the law of products liability are part of the impressive array of substantive changes of tort law occurring at an accelerated pace during the decade commencing in 1958. The new law of products liability deserves special attention because of its wide scope of application and the even greater scope of its potential influence on basic principles of liability.

Perhaps we should speak not of a new products liability, but of products liabilities, in the plural, for the new cases disclose not one but an array of somewhat inconsistent theories, with no dominant choice yet clear. In such a formative period as this, it is especially relevant to ask: What is the general impact on tort law, practical and theoretical, of the varied ideas of products liabilities advanced in judicial opinions and elsewhere? This is the primary perspective from which these developments are considered here.

THE GREENMAN AND GOLDBERG CASES

Two decisions of early 1963 mark an undisputed breakthrough for a new doctrine.

In *Greenman v. Yuba Power Products, Inc.*,[1] a plaintiff sued the retailer and manufacturer of a combination power tool known as a Shopsmith. It could be used as a saw, drill, and wood lathe. And it turned out to be even more versatile. In the language of a New York judge, describing this California case, the machine in question "threw a piece of wood at a user." [2] If that suggests machines revolting against their masters, perhaps less disturbing is the description by the California court, deciding the case. As they put it, personifying the wood rather than the machine, a piece of wood the user wished to make into a chalice "suddenly flew out of the machine and struck him on the forehead, inflicting serious injuries." The Shopsmith had been bought by the user's wife and given to him for Christmas in 1955. In 1957 he had purchased the necessary attachments to use it as a lathe for turning a large piece of wood such as he was working with at the time of injury. Said the California court, "To establish the manufacturer's liability it was sufficient that plaintiff proved that he was injured while using the Shopsmith in a way it was intended to be used as a result of a defect in design and manufacture of which plaintiff was not aware that made the Shopsmith unsafe for its intended use."

In the New York case, *Goldberg v. Kollsman Instrument Corporation*,[3] Chief Judge Desmond, writing for the majority, posed the question for decision in somewhat different terms. "The question now to be answered is: does a manufacturer's implied warranty of fitness of his product for its contemplated use run in favor of all its intended users,

[1] 59 Cal. 2d 57, 377 P.2d 897, 27 Cal. Rptr. 697 (1963), 13 A.L.R.3d 1049 (1967).
[2] Goldberg v. Kollsman Instrument Corp., 12 N.Y.2d 432, 437, 191 N.E.2d 81, 83, 240 N.Y.S.2d 592, 595 (1963).
[3] 12 N.Y.2d 432, 191 N.E.2d 81, 240 N.Y.S.2d 592 (1963).

despite lack of privity of contract?" It is a more generalized statement of the issue with respect to products to which it extends, and more generalized in the sense that it is stated not in terms of the facts of the particular case but rather as a generally applicable proposition. Yet it too is cautiously particularized in some respects, and arguably even more so than the phrasing of the California court. Note the focus on the privity question. Note the use of the terminology of implied warranty. And note that the question concerns "all its intended users" rather than more broadly applying to all who might foreseeably be injured by use of the product.

The majority answered their question in the affirmative. The decision would be important if that were the whole story. But it is the more important and interesting because of further details.

The suit was by an administratrix for the death of her daughter as the result of injuries suffered in the crash of an American Airlines flight near La Guardia Airport. The deceased was a fare-paying passenger. American, owner and operator of the plane, was sued along with Kollsman Instrument and Lockheed Aircraft on the theory of negligence, but on this appeal the negligence theory was not before the court. Plaintiff also sued Kollsman (manufacturer and supplier of the plane's altimeter) and Lockheed (assembler of the plane) for breach of their respective implied warranties of merchantability and fitness. It was from the dismissal of these causes of action in implied warranty that the plaintiff appealed. The questions placed before the court in this setting were legal questions arising on the factual assumption of a defect in the plane's altimeter. At this juncture the question whether in fact a defective altimeter was responsible for the crash was not up for decision.[4]

[4] For an unofficial story of the crash, strongly suggesting that it may not have been caused by a defective altimeter, see Hunt, "The Case of Flight 320," *The New Yorker* 36:119 (April 30, 1960).

Despite the safeguards courts employ to decide real and not hypothetical issues, a landmark decision can be based on rather imaginative claims about the facts. Compare the celebrated case of Palsgraf v. Long Island R.R., 248 N.Y. 339, 162 N.E. 99 (1928) (opinion by Cardozo). As defendant's employees tried to help a passenger who was boarding a train already in motion, a "package of small size" containing fireworks was dislodged from the passenger's grasp and fell on the rails, exploding; "some scales at the other end of the platform, many feet away," fell on the plaintiff, causing injury. It was supposed that the "shock of the explosion threw down" the scales. Recovery was denied because the conduct of the defendant's guards, if a wrong to the holder of the package, was not a wrong to the plaintiff, "standing far away," since "nothing in the situation gave notice" of "peril to persons thus removed."

The New York court cited with approval the California decision on the Shopsmith and adopted essentially the same line of reasoning—approving as a statement of the purpose of such holding the objective of seeing to it "that the costs of injuries resulting from defective products are borne by the manufacturers who put the products on the market rather than by injured persons who are powerless to protect themselves." This significant proposition was added: "However, for the present at least we do not think it necessary so to extend this rule as to hold liable the manufacturer (defendant Kollsman) of a component part. Adequate protection is provided for the passengers by casting in liability the airplane manufacturer which put into the market the completed aircraft." Thus, dismissal as to Kollsman was affirmed, while dismissal as to Lockheed was reversed.

Three judges dissented. They pointed out that this case did not fall within any of the implied warranty precedents of the state. They asserted that the majority, if choosing to impose strict products or enterprise liability, could not escape the responsibility of justifying it. The dissenters found unacceptable the implication they saw in the majority opinion that the difference between warranty and strict products liability is merely one of phrasing. They challenged the wisdom of this extension of liability. They noted that risks of air travel are well known and flight insurance is available. They also called attention to the fact that under the precedents, the measure of American Airlines' duty toward the deceased was an undertaking of reasonably safe carriage, discharged by the use of due care. "Crucial is the fact that this duty would be unaffected if American assembled its own planes, even if they contained a latent defect," the dissent asserted. Incidentally, we may doubt that American's duty is now unaffected if it assembles its own planes, even if unaffected according to the law as it stood before *Kollsman*.

The dissenting judges also observed that they could "see no satisfactory basis on which to uphold against Lockheed a cause of action not grounded in negligence, while disallowing it against the manufacturer of an alleged defective part." Their opinion suggested further that the enterprise to which accidents such as this are more appropriately charged is the carriage of passengers by air: American's enterprise. It is the dominant enterprise, and the one with which the deceased did business. The dissenters also expressed doubt about whether in practice matters would work out in conformity with the theory that the enterprise on which the burden is imposed will be able to distribute the cost among its consumers—particularly when a closely regulated business such as air carriage is involved. The conclusion to which all this built, in their opinion, was that the whole matter was one for a legislature rather than a court.

Even if one does not agree with that conclusion, he is likely to find some of the points made by the dissent quite cogent, particularly in relation to choosing a target for strict products liability.

WHOSE LIABILITY?

The special twist that the majority in *Goldberg* gave to the doctrine of strict products liability by imposing such liability on Lockheed only, and not upon either Kollsman or American, seems a particular source of difficulty. Saying that the airline passenger and his representatives need no more protection than an action against Lockheed is hardly a good answer to the question whether Lockheed or Kollsman or American or all of them should be subject to the strict liability. The dissenting opinion made some point of the fact that precedents limited the liability of American to negligence. Perhaps the majority took their particular course of imposing liability on Lockheed only in deference to those precedents. Also, some amendment of the pleadings might have been necessary in the case sub judice, since the plaintiff's theory of strict products liability, or implied warranty, was alleged against Kollsman and Lockheed but not against American.

As to choosing which among the various persons in the chain of manufacture and marketing shall be subject to strict liability for injury a product causes, there is a curious and interesting comparison between the views of the New York court in *Goldberg* and the views developed in a sequence of Texas cases involving impure foods. One Texas case held the manufacturer of the impure food subject to strict liability.[5] Another case held the retailer liable.[6] And in a third case, *Bowman v. Hines Biscuit Co.*,[7] a closely divided court held a wholesaler *not* subject to strict liability.

Does this mean that in Texas the man in the middle is safe and those on each flank are exposed, but in New York the man in the middle is liable and those on each flank are safe? Perhaps the precedents in these

[5] Jacob E. Decker & Sons, Inc., v. Capps, 139 Tex. 609, 164 S.W.2d 828 (1942).

[6] Griggs Canning Co. v. Josey, 139 Tex. 623, 164 S.W.2d 835 (1942).

[7] 151 Tex. 370, 251 S.W.2d 153 (1952).

two states can be reconciled on the ground that when the middleman is the assembler, as in *Goldberg*, he has potential control over the defect, whereas if he is merely a merchandising channel, as in *Bowman*, others in the chain of marketing may be better targets for responsibility. But should we distinguish the New York and Texas cases and attempt to sustain both rules, or should one or both rules be changed?

In a case like *Goldberg*, if one were writing on a clean slate, or were legislating with no concern about the propriety of his role as legislator, surely he would be more likely to pick American than Lockheed as the proper enterprise—if he felt obliged to pick. Perhaps even more likely would be a refusal to choose among three parties situated as were Kollsman, Lockheed, and American—a determination, in short, that the principle of strict liability is good against all three enterprises in this chain that released a defective product. The best of the arguments for liability of the assembler on the theory of responsibility for the defect because of control over the product at some point along the way seem applicable with at least equal force against the maker of the altimeter. The best of the arguments for liability of the assembler on the theory of risk-spreading capacity and allocation of costs to consumers seem applicable with at least equal force against the airlines. Why pick the assembler? It seems more likely, and more defensible, that the courts will decline to become embroiled in distinguishing among three involved parties in situations of this kind, and will instead hold that the rule of strict liability applies against all three.

Who eventually bears the cost of payment made to victims under strict products liability? This question may be answered temporarily by contracts among the various entities involved in bringing the product to the consumer. Claims for indemnity or contribution are subject to contractual modification, and such contracts are likely to be made in a high percentage of cases, at least after the doctrine of strict products liability becomes well known. Indeed, such contracts will be likely to determine the secondary impact regardless of the victim's or the court's choice of one or another entity as an immediate target of strict liability, unless there is a supplemental rule declaring it against public policy to modify by contract the incidence of this liability.

Whichever entity pays the victim will ordinarily wish to pass the cost forward toward the consumer or backward toward some supplier. The first supplier against whom any effort is plausible will resist with greater vigor since the only direction in which he can pass the cost is forward. Thus, the pressure is stronger in general for passing costs forward. If the economic market is fully responsive to this pressure, the full burden eventually rests on the consumers of the product, because it is reflected in the price they must pay.

This is not to say that the doctrinal choice about who in the chain of marketing is subject to strict liability is unimportant as long as somebody is held responsible. Rather, that choice may be highly significant. The economic market is never such that the cost will be passed along without decrease or increment. If the cost is initially placed on the entity corresponding with Kollsman in the chain of marketing, it may be that none or only part of it eventually is passed along through the entities corresponding with Lockheed and American to the consumer, the airline passenger. Or it may be that the cost is passed along with an increment at each stage so that the consumer pays more than he would have paid if the cost had been placed initially on the entity nearest him in the chain. Perhaps some increment should be expected as the norm since the transmission itself always involves administrative expense.

A second reason for significance of the choice about which one or more of the entities in the chain of marketing will be subject to strict liability is that the victim's success in recovering compensation depends on financial responsibility as well as liability. If only one entity in the chain of marketing is subject to liability to the victim, and that one is financially irresponsible, it is no comfort to the victim to know that he has a theoretically valid claim against one defendant. Nor is this comfort for the economic planner who intends the eventual impact of strict products liability to be reflected in the price of the product. Both the victim and the planner are frustrated by the financial irresponsibility of the sole entity subject to strict liability.

These observations lend strong support to a rule that subjects to the principle of strict liability not one but all of the entities in the chain of marketing. The rule might properly be qualified, however, to excuse those whose connection with the marketing of the product is distinctively attenuated—a type of qualification commonly stated as a legal cause requirement. It may be noted too that these observations support the application of such a broadly inclusive rule regardless of how arrangements are worked out for passing along costs, either by contract, or by the enforcement of rights of indemnity or contribution apart from contract.

THE REQUIREMENT OF A DEFECT

In different ways, each of these two leading decisions—*Greenman* in the California court and *Goldberg* in the New York court—requires a showing that the harm of which the plaintiff complains was caused by some shortcoming of the product. The California court in stating its rule of decision speaks of the plaintiff's proving "that he was injured . . . as a result of a defect in design and manufacture of which plaintiff was not aware that made the Shopsmith unsafe for its intended use." [8] The New York court in stating the question to be answered speaks of "a manufacturer's implied warranty of fitness of his product for its contemplated use." [9]

These two methods of expression are aimed at stating the same kind of requirement. This has come to be discussed generally as the requirement of a defect; [10] before 1963, it was more often referred to as a requirement of unfitness. The change of expression came about because of the general shift to talking about strict products liability in contrast with the previous custom of talking about implied warranty. We will return later to the question whether this change in way of speaking is a substantive as well as a linguistic change. For the moment, the relevant point is that the change in general terminology has carried with it a change in terminology about a product's shortcoming, since "unfitness" is associated with implied warranty and "defectiveness" is associated with strict products liability. There are differences among jurisdictions about the substantive requirement concerning the shortcomings of the product, but they seem not to correlate with the differences in terminology. Thus, it seems appropriate to choose one or the other terminology for convenience without intending substantive implications. The term "defect" and its derivatives will be used here.

Cases thus far reported present not one but several subtheories concerning what constitutes a defect sufficient to support a strict products liability.

At one extreme are cases like *Lartigue*,[11] in which it was the task of

[8] 59 Cal. 2d at 64, 377 P.2d at 901, 27 Cal. Rptr. at 701.

[9] 12 N.Y.2d at 434–435, 191 N.E.2d at 81, 240 N.Y.S.2d at 593.

[10] See, for example, Dickerson, "Products Liability: How Good Does A Product Have to Be?" 42 *Ind. L. J.* 301 (1967); Dickerson, "The Basis of Strict Products Liability," 17 *Bus. Law* 157, 166 (1961), published also in 16 *Food Drug Cosm. L. J.* 585, 595 (1961); Page Keeton, "Products Liability—Liability Without Fault and the Requirement of a Defect," 41 *Texas L. Rev.* 855 (1963).

[11] Lartigue v. R. J. Reynolds Tobacco Co., 317 F.2d 19 (5th Cir. 1963).

the Court of Appeals for the Fifth Circuit, under *Erie* doctrine,[12] to apply state law. The court concluded that under Louisiana law "a manufacturer of food and cigarettes is strictly liable for foreseeable harm resulting from a defective condition in the product when the consumer uses the product for the purposes for which it was manufactured and marketed." But they affirmed a judgment on a general verdict for the defendants. It was their best estimate of Louisiana law that, for liability to be imposed, the product "must be unreasonably dangerous to the ordinary consumer, with the knowledge common to the community as to its characterization." Proof that cigarettes contribute to cancer does not necessarily establish that they are defective or unwholesome in the sense required for strict liability, or negligence liability either, for that matter. This court held that Louisiana law requires a showing that the harm-causing characteristic be one that could reasonably be foreseen by the manufacturer of the product—in that case cigarettes. That showing they found not to have been made; that is, the plaintiff did not show that, at the time of marketing the tobacco smoked by plaintiff's deceased husband, the requisite information about the relation between tobacco and lung cancer was available to the manufacturer.

Arguably there is some difference between requiring proof of a defect in this sense and requiring proof that the manufacturer was negligent, but the difference is slight in theory, and perhaps even slighter in practical impact. Virtually the same evidence is likely to be marshaled on either issue, and it seems unlikely that juries would often respond differently to the slightly contrasting charges that would be given.

The defendant won also in *Casagrande v. F. W. Woolworth Co.*[13] It appeared that the plaintiff suffered from dermatitis after application of a deodorant purchased from the defendant. The court held that the plaintiff failed to meet her burden of showing that the product was unfit—"that is, that it would have sensitized [and injured] a significant number of persons . . . either immediately or after a period of use." Thus, one may find in a particular case that the defect—the aberration —is not in the defendant's product but in the plaintiff's skin.

These two cases serve to illustrate the point that the new strict products liability is not nearly as horrendous in scope and impact as some have feared. Indeed, in some jurisdictions, at least, it is a very modest

12 Erie R.R. v. Tompkins, 304 U.S. 64 (1938).
13 340 Mass. 552, 165 N.E.2d 109 (1960).

extension of liability, since in many types of cases one who could prove defect could usually find a defendant against whom res ipsa loquitur would aid him to secure a verdict based on negligence.

The new §402A of the American Law Institute's *Restatement of Torts (Second)*, a tentative version of which was cited in the *Lartigue* opinion, approves the requirement of a defect and supports the requirement that the product be "unreasonably dangerous" to the ordinary consumer. It is debatable whether this standard means for cigarette cases or any others that to prove the product defective one must show that the manufacturer or other person allegedly accountable could have known about the defect in the exercise of reasonable care. The translation of the standard in *Lartigue* as requiring such proof arguably is a more rigorous requirement than most courts will impose. Only if cigarette cases are distinguished—for example, because of the uncertain state of scientific knowledge about causes of lung cancer, or because of the publicity given to such learning on the subject as is available—can *Lartigue* be regarded as no more stringent in its requirement of defect than the general tendency of the strict liability decisions. A panel of the same United States Court of Appeals took a very different view when undertaking to apply the law of Florida, as they understood it, to the cigarette-cancer problem.[14]

At the opposite extreme from a formidable standard requiring one to prove that the manufacturer or other accountable entity could have known about the defect in the exercise of reasonable care, it has been argued that no defect should be required—that a product should pay its way by paying for all the injuries it causes. This argument is generally rejected, but a few impure food decisions approach very near this position by classifying food products as defective because containing impurities that other courts have regarded as natural to the product.[15]

On the basis of such precedents it has been argued, for example, that the producer of fish chowder should be liable for harm caused by an occasional piece of bone even though from time immemorial fish chowder of the finest quality—New England fish chowder—has been known to contain such fragments. In this instance there is no defect in the sense of deviation from what is in fact common. The Supreme Judicial Court of Massachusetts has understandably refused to character-

14 Green v. American Tobacco Co., 391 F.2d 97 (5th Cir. 1968).
15 For example, Betehia v. Cape Cod Corp., 10 Wis. 2d 323, 103 N.W.2d 64 (1960) (jury question whether a chicken bone in a chicken sandwich is a defect).

ize fish chowder as defective merely because it conforms with this ro-
bust quality.[16] The argument arises also with respect to unwanted sea-
soning in other culinary delights—a partially crystallized grain of corn
in corn flakes,[17] pinto beans with an occasional pebble of like color to
the beans but rather different texture, and fried oysters [18] or oyster
stew with an occasional piece of shell or perhaps even a pearl worthy
of a better fate than being delivered as a bonus and especially to a consumer who has neither won a contest nor collected stamps. No doubt
the argument for characterizing the food as defective is strongest in the
case of the pearl and, curiously, grows stronger still with its size and
rarity.

The argument that no requirement of defect should be imposed has
been advanced, too, in relation to drugs. Suppose a new drug that has
wondrous properties for healing certain ills, but also grave dangers to
that segment of the population for whose welfare judges, and even
more so law professors and students, have long been notably solicitous
—that is, pregnant women. Of course if the drug is marketed without
adequate warning of this dangerous characteristic, it (or at least the
marketing unit composed of it and the instructions that go with it) is
plainly defective. On the other hand, if adequate warning is given, the
argument for calling this characteristic of the drug a defect for products liability purposes is weak indeed. If this makes the drug defective,
then as Judges Goodrich and Wisdom have taught us, surely sugar is
defective because of its propensity for harm to diabetics and whiskey
because of its propensity for harm to alcoholics.[19]

Defendants have available another framework of theory to fortify
the requirement of defect—consent or assumption of risk. When one is
fully informed of the risky characteristic of the product and makes an
informed choice to use it, the case for assumption of risk is about as
strong as it can ever be. Even in the present low state of esteem for
that doctrine, it should be expected to prevail in this kind of case unless the court insists on reaching the same result for another reason
such as lack of proof of a defect.

[16] Webster v. Blue Ship Tea Room, Inc., 347 Mass. 421, 198 N.E.2d 309
(1964).

[17] For example, Adams v. Great Atl. & Pac. Tea Co., 251 N.C. 565, 112 S.E.2d
92 (1960).

[18] For example, Allen v. Grafton, 170 Ohio St. 249, 164 N.E.2d 167 (1960).

[19] Lartigue v. R. J. Reynolds Tobacco Co., 317 F.2d 19, 37 (5th Cir. 1963);
Pritchard v. Liggett & Myers Tobacco Co., 295 F.2d 292, 302 (3d Cir. 1961).

A number of problems, inherent in the requirement of defect, will continue to provoke debate as precedents accumulate. The following are examples.

Is the manufacturer of a product held accountable for all that is discoverable, or all that is known among the best scientists and researchers, for example, or only for what the industry by custom has taken account of, or only what ordinary prudent persons exercising reasonable care in an industry position would know?

Is a manufacturer of a product liable for failure to spend more in research than it has spent, with the consequence that a judge or jury may be permitted to say that a safety feature developed at a given time should have been developed earlier—that the product without the safety feature was defective? A suit arising from the crash of a propeller-driven airplane without Pitch Lock, a device to prevent overspeeding, was decided on grounds that left this question open to debate.[20] The device had actually been placed in use on other types of planes and without doubt could have been available for installation in the plane that came to be destroyed in this crash had more time and money been committed to research and development for this purpose. A finding of negligence of the manufacturer was sustained, but arguably on the ground not of tardy development but that a fully developed and available device was not used.

THE EFFECT OF DISCLAIMERS

The possibility of contractual modification of liability is relevant not only to distribution of the burden of strict liability among entities in the chain of marketing but also to the right of the injured person to recover against any entity with which he has had contractual dealings.

The New Jersey court in the *Henningsen* case [21] applied the theory of strict liability against an automobile dealer as well as the manufacturer of the defective automobile. The contract of purchase contained exculpatory clauses in the so-called standard automobile manufacturers warranty. These the court struck down as contrary to public policy.

The majority decision in *Goldberg*, imposing liability on Lockheed (an entity in the middle of the chain of marketing) rather than American (with whom the consumer dealt), bypasses for most cases this

---

[20] Noel v. United Aircraft Corp., 342 F.2d 232 (3d Cir. 1965).
[21] Henningsen v. Bloomfield Motors, Inc., 32 N.J. 358, 161 A.2d 69 (1960), 75 A.L.R.2d 1 (1961).

problem of policing exculpatory clauses. But the problem can still arise, even under such a rule placing liability on an entity in the middle of the chain. For example, it can still arise in automobile transactions, since manufacturers (who, like Lockheed, are assemblers) often insist that dealers make contracts with exculpatory clauses purportedly benefiting the manufacturers.

Before *Henningsen,* there was little precedent anywhere for disregarding the exculpatory clauses of the automobile manufacturers warranty. Since that decision, a number of other courts have joined the New Jersey court in declaring these provisions unenforceable.[22] One reason given is the unequal bargaining power of the individual purchaser, on the one hand, and the manufacturer and dealer on the other. A second reason is the repugnance of these clauses to the generous claims advanced by manufacturers in national advertising of their products. A few decisions since *Henningsen* have continued to sustain these exculpatory provisions,[23] however, with the result that in some states it is still true that the so-called warranty offered by automobile manufacturers takes away more than it gives; the automobile purchaser would be better off without it. The more manufacturers say in their national advertising about the expansion of their warranties, however, the stronger case they build coincidentally for wider adoption of the *Henningsen* rule of invalidity of the exculpatory fine print on the second of the grounds just stated: misleading advertisements that paint the warranty as generous and helpful, without disclosing its rather stunning restrictions.

If a claimant cannot succeed in a direct assault against the validity of an exculpatory clause, he may nevertheless reach the desired destination by an end run. One way around a disclaimer is to sue upon a theory of misrepresentation. Support can be found for strict liability (that is, liability even for innocent misrepresentation) not only as to personal injury and property damage [24] but also as to nonphysical economic loss.[25] It might be argued for the defense that a disclaimer in the pur-

[22] For example, Seely v. White Motor Co., 63 Cal. 2d 9, 403 P.2d 145, 45 Cal. Rptr. 17 (1965); State Farm Mut. Auto. Ins. Co. v. Anderson-Weber, Inc., 252 Iowa 1289, 110 N.W.2d 449 (1961). See *Restatement (Second), Torts,* § 496B (1965); Annot., 99 A.L.R.2d 1419 (1965).

[23] For example, Payne v. Valley Motor Sales, Inc., 124 S.E.2d 622 (W. Va. 1962).

[24] For example, *Restatement (Second), Torts,* § 402B (1965).

[25] Ford Motor Co. v. Lonon, 398 S.W.2d 240 (Tenn. 1966). A manufacturer of farm equipment was held liable under the theory of *Restatement*

chase contract was intended to preclude liability on this theory as well as any theory of express or implied warranty or strict products liability. But the claimant is aided by rules of construction disfavoring an interpretation that relieves one of liability for misrepresentation, at least if it was intended or negligent misrepresentation, and especially if the party asserting the disclaimer was responsible for drafting the questioned clause.

A second way around a disclaimer is sometimes available because some representative of the party asserting the disclaimer participates in efforts to satisfy the claimant. If, for example, an automobile manufacturer's representative participates in efforts by the dealer to correct a defect in a vehicle purchased by the claimant, and later the manufacturer asserts that its liability is limited by the terms of the disclaimer to making good defective parts at the factory, the claimant may reasonably argue an estoppel. He may say the manufacturer misled him by not insisting on the terms of the disclaimer.[26] In light of a background of unequal bargaining power, it may happen that the requirements the claimant must meet are not as rigorous as those of a strict estoppel theory under which the claimant would be protected only to the extent of detrimental reliance on the manufacturer's misleading conduct.

THE RELATION BETWEEN IMPLIED WARRANTY AND STRICT PRODUCTS LIABILITY; THE EFFECT OF LEGISLATION

During the quarter century before the era of strict products liability was ushered in by the California and New York courts, the way was being prepared by decisions that gradually increased the scope of liability without negligence—first in food cases, then in cases of drugs for internal and next for external use. All the while there was increasing uneasiness about the distinction between being injured by consuming pieces of a decomposed mouse or cockroach in a bottled carbonated beverage (for which liability without negligence was generally al-

---

(*Second*), *Torts*, § 402B, to a farmer-purchaser for commercial loss because the equipment was defective and failed to measure up to the manufacturer's representations; § 402A was not applied because there was no showing that the equipment was unreasonably dangerous as well as defective.

[26] Compare Seely v. White Motor Co., 63 Cal. 2d 9, 17, 403 P.2d 145, 151, 45 Cal. Rptr. 17, 23 (1965): "Defendant is liable only because of its agreement as defined by its continuing practice over 11 months. Without an agreement, defined by practice or otherwise, defendant should not be liable for these commercial losses" (including lost profits and the refund of money paid for a defective truck used in the plaintiff's business).

lowed) and being injured by flying glass from explosion of the bottle (for which negligence was generally essential to the claim). Before 1963, a number of decisions had pushed this further distance of allowing liability without negligence for injury from fragments of the container, and a few the added distance to other products.[27] In general all these decisions in food, drug, and bottle cases proceeded on a theory of implied warranty of fitness for human consumption. Moreover, in a figure of speech common in legal discourse and nicely descriptive in this instance, these implied warranties sound in contract.

One can argue, as was often done, that an implied warranty is an imposed liability, of the character of tort, rather than a consensually based liability, of the character of contract. But the word warranty itself connotes a contractual transaction: a sale. And the draftsmen of commercial legislation—sales acts initially and the Uniform Commercial Code (UCC) more recently—undertook to say, at the least, something about implied warranties. Did they say enough to impinge substantially on the freedom courts would otherwise have had to reconsider and revise decisional doctrines that had required negligence to sustain liability for various types of harm, including personal injury, caused by defective products other than those intended for human consumption?

One aspect of this inquiry is whether such legislation precludes courts from applying a doctrine of strict products liability in areas not covered by such a doctrine when the legislation was enacted. For example, does such legislation preclude courts from extending strict products liability to all kinds of products? Relatively little support can be found for the position that either the UCC or earlier commercial legislation was designed to effect such a freeze regarding the basis of liability. A second aspect of the problem has proved to be more controversial. Should such legislation be held to require courts, whenever they choose to apply a doctrine of strict products liability, to adhere to all the statutory provisions concerning such things as notice of claim, privity, and effectiveness of disclaimers?

Since the Uniform Commercial Code has now been widely adopted, its provisions on these subjects are of potentially great significance. One view on this controversial issue is that the provisions of the UCC concerning notice of claim, privity, effectiveness of disclaimer, and the

---

[27] See *Restatement* (*Second*), *Torts,* § 402A, and cases collected in the Reporter's Notes to § 402A (Appendix, 1966).

like apply to the new theory of strict products liability. Protagonists of this view have sharply criticized judicial opinions, *Restatement* drafts, and various other writings for allegedly disregarding these code provisions in their expositions of strict products liability.

This is not to say that adherents of the view that these code provisions apply to strict products liability contend generally that the provisions were wisely drafted for this application or that they were deliberately designed to inhibit development of broader liabilities for harms caused by defective products. Indeed, it is commonly agreed that draftsmen of the code considered that their provisions would tend to have a liberalizing rather than an inhibiting influence on the scope of liability. But they did not anticipate the sharp changes in the decisional law of products liability that occurred almost simultaneously with widespread enactment of the code. In this context the code occupies the role of an inhibiting influence if it applies. The code provisions, if they apply, allow procedural and contractual defenses not commonly available to a defendant sued on a tort theory—whether it be negligence or strict liability. Thus, one way of framing the question presented is to ask whether a court that is admittedly and openly changing the law of liability for harms caused by defective products is precluded by the code from declaring that procedural and contractual defenses ordinarily unavailable in tort cases shall also be unavailable here.

Of course we should face this issue on the merits, and not by merely labeling the action as tort or contract and then applying the rules normally associated with that label. On this everyone agrees. But, as one might expect, those who favor applicability of the code sometimes accuse their opposition of arguing nothing more substantial than labels for pigeonholing in tort (that is, strict products liability rather than implied warranty of fitness). Conversely, those disfavoring the code provisions accuse their opposition of arguing nothing more substantial than labels for pigeonholing in contract.

On the merits, this is a question of statutory interpretation. Does the UCC apply and, if so, what is the legislature's mandate on this issue?

What in general was the core problem the UCC was designed to meet and what kinds of activities, primarily, was it designed to regulate? Is it not the case that the problem in general was one of commerce, and that commercial transactions, at least primarily, were the activities to be regulated?

Claims for personal injuries and property damages arising from accidents come into fairly close relation with transactions of commerce in some situations, however, because harms are sometimes caused by defective articles of commerce. Thus these claims bear a relation to, if they are not within, the primary concern of the UCC. It would have been possible, then, for the code draftsmen to think of these claims as closely enough related to their primary concern to be part of the area for which they should prescribe. But by no means were they inescapably compelled to reach that conclusion. The problem of statutory construction is reasonably debatable not alone on the basis of the language appearing in various sections of the UCC but also from this perspective of general purpose.

The primary concern of the law of strict products liability stands in contrast with the primary concern of the code. In the law of strict products liability, as in the law of negligence, the foremost concern is the regulation of compensation for accidental harm to person and property. Here again the disputed area is beyond the primary concern. Commercial transactions bear a relation to claims for accidental harm to person and property, since articles of commerce are in the chain of causation, but the commercial transactions themselves are not within the primary concern of this area of law. Are they nevertheless to be regulated by judicially developed doctrines designed to implement the policies underlying the judicially developed strict products liability?

As a way of examining the relation between these areas of law, it may be useful to observe the different types of claims for harms arising in some sense from defective products. They might be arrayed as follows.

First, accidental injuries to person—as in the cases of the driver, passenger, and pedestrian injured when a car with a defective steering mechanism crashes.

Second, accidental damage to property other than the defective product itself—as in the case of damage to another car struck by a car out of control because of a defective steering mechanism.

Third, accidental damage to the defective product itself—as in the case of damage to the car when it crashes because of a defective steering mechanism.

Fourth, unexpectedly low value of the product itself to an ordinary consumer because of characteristics that develop or are revealed gradually rather than by a sudden event such as is implied by the term "accidental." An example is presented in the claim of a householder against a carpet manufacturer seeking recovery of damages because a carpet that was represented to be of good quality, evenly resistant to wear, actually wore in streaks.[28]

Fifth, nonphysical harms to an ordinary consumer, including both economic losses and pain and suffering, arising because a product does not measure up to expectations. An example is presented in the claim of a purchaser of what is commonly referred to as a "lemon"—an automobile whose defects not only deprive the purchaser of the value of use of the vehicle itself but also cause him anxiety, mental distress, and expenses for substitute transportation. When associated with accidental harms to person or property, these kinds of losses are sometimes held compensable under rubrics of legal cause and parasitic damages. This fifth category, in contrast, concerns harms sustained without associated physical harm.

Sixth, unexpectedly low value of the product itself to a commercial purchaser as distinguished from an ordinary consumer. An example is presented in the claim of a retailer of carpets against the supplier from whom he purchased them, based on the fact that they proved to be of lower quality and less salable than the retailer had expected.

Seventh, reduction in value of other property because of its association with the product in question in some commercial context. An example is presented in the claim against a synthetics manufacturer by the manufacturer of hula skirts rendered valueless because it turned out that the synthetic substitute for grass used in making them would burst into uncontrollable flame on contact with a source of heat, such as a lighted cigarette, thus endowing an artistic routine with a more explosive quality than could reasonably have been anticipated. Note that the harm in this category is not fire damage—which would fall in the first, second, or third category, depending on what was damaged —but loss of value of a stock of hula skirts because of the risk of fire.

Eighth, nonphysical economic losses arising in a commercial context because the product does not measure up to expectations. An example is presented in the claim of a commercial purchaser of equipment for loss of expected profits caused by the failure of the equipment to perform in the expected way.

Plainly arguments about whether a claim falls within the area regulated by the UCC have greatly differing cogency in relation to some

[28] Santor v. A & M Karagheusian, Inc., 44 N.J. 52, 207 A.2d 305 (1965), 16 A.L.R.3d 670 (1967).

among these different classes of claims. This would be conceded, perhaps, even by those who would argue at one extreme that UCC provisions apply to all eight classes [29] or, at what appears to be as near to the other extreme as any argument is likely to prevail, that they apply only to the sixth, seventh, and eighth categories.[30]

What is the best answer to this problem of statutory interpretation? What help might we get from the guidelines to statutory interpretation suggested in Chapter 6? The initial question as formulated there is whether the legislature enacting the UCC, or the draftsmen on whom they depended, considered the problem with which the court is concerned and prescribed an answer. If so, the court should apply the answer prescribed in the UCC. If not, the court should formulate its own answer; in doing so, however, it should seek one that relates reasonably to those provided in the code.

Did the legislature enacting the code, or the draftsmen on whom they depended, consider and prescribe for the set of problems the courts face in expanding the area of strict products liability?

Perhaps it is instructive to consider the state of the law on liabilities for harms caused by defective products during the period when the code was being formulated and enacted in the first states to adopt it. Although there were forecasts of later developments, it seems fair to describe the existing law at that time as providing for three independent bases of liability, with differing requisites and differing but overlapping scope—and the fact of overlapping may be quite significant. Of course there was also the associated negative rule that no recovery would be allowed if the plaintiff could not bring his claim within any of these three rules.

One of the three bases of liability—implied warranty of products intended for human consumption—effected liability without negligence for personal injuries accidentally caused by unfitness of products intended for human consumption (part of the first category above) but no liability in other cases (the rest of the first and all other categories). The second basis of liability provided for recovery upon proof of neg-

[29] See, for example, Franklin, "When Worlds Collide: Liability Theories and Disclaimers in Defective-Product Cases," 18 *Stan. L. Rev.* 974 (1966); Shanker, "Strict Tort Theory of Products Liability and the Uniform Commercial Code: A Commentary on Jurisprudential Eclipses, Pigeonholes and Communication Barriers," 17 *W. Res. L. Rev.* 5 (1965).

[30] See Santor v. A & M Karagheusian, Inc., 44 N.J. 52, 207 A.2d 305 (1965), 16 A.L.R.3d 670 (1967), which appears to push as far toward this extreme as any decision to date.

ligence, but not otherwise, for all kinds of physical harms accidentally caused by defects in products, whether or not intended for human consumption (the first three of the eight categories above), but no liability in other cases (the fourth through eighth categories). The third basis of liability, a group of theories of express and implied warranties of merchantability and fitness for contemplated use, provided remedies sometimes—but subject to many qualifications contractual, decisional, and statutory—at least for some harms and losses within each of the fourth through the eighth categories, and perhaps in some states for those within the first three categories as well.

Did the draftsmen of the UCC have in mind a fourth basis of liability: strict products liability in cases of at least the first three categories described above—that is, accidental harms caused by defects in all kinds of products whether intended for human consumption or not? Were they adverting to such a theory of liability when drafting the various UCC provisions about notice of claim, privity, disclaimer, and the like? Surely the correct answer is the negative. But that is not a complete answer to the problem of interpreting and applying the statute, since a court should seek to formulate doctrines with conscious concern for avoiding unreasonable distinctions when answering questions that are beyond the core of the statutory prescription but are in substantial degree analogous. Thus there is need to consider the nature of the analogy.

If one thinks of the new liability as an extension applying to other products the rule of implied warranty previously applied to products for human consumption, he is pressed toward the conclusion that the analogy is so close that the court ought to apply the UCC rules to this new liability. But one may also think of the new liability as a modest extension of negligence law, which had been achieving the result of liability in most cases of harms from defective products, especially in view of the practical effect of allowing the injured person to get to a jury verdict under the theory of res ipsa loquitur by proving harm from a defect, without any specific evidence as to how the defect came to be in the product. Or he may think of the new liability as a modest extension of ideas of fault or unjust enrichment underlying negligence law. From these perspectives, the new area of liability is at least as much like negligence liability as like implied warranty.

Take still another perspective. It might be said that when the UCC was being drafted there were these pertinent rules in most states: first,

liability based on negligence whether the product was one inten(
human consumption or not; second, liability without negligence
case of products intended for human consumption; third, nonl:
for cases of accidental harm not involving either negligence o1
ucts intended for human consumption. As previously noted, it *
to be generally agreed that the UCC did not undertake to *precl*
dicial recognition of liability without negligence in cases of othe
ucts. Why, then, should the UCC be interpreted as *regulating* s
tensions of liability? Should it not be the case, instead, that the
free to formulate the details of the new liability, which falls in tl
not covered by the other two theories (or covered in a negative
that nonliability was their prescription), and that it is free to d(
cording to whichever pattern it considers more appropriate, or
according to a new pattern not exactly like either of the oth(
course the court should be concerned that no unreasonable disti
occur—that no lack of evenhandedness occur as it draws lines b
cases dealt with under the different patterns. But that is a task ir
the statute is treated not as a mandate covering the new area b
datum with respect to treatment of cases bearing some simi
which datum is to be taken into account in constructing the nev
ity so the correlation is reasonable and fair.

Two points of view advanced in the majority and dissentin
ions, respectively, in the *Seely* case,[31] decided in California i
are relevant to this problem. The case involved a truck manuf;
by the defendant and purchased by the plaintiff through a
Plaintiff found that the truck "galloped"—that is, it bounded v
in use. For eleven months, with guidance of the defendant's re
tatives, the dealer made unsuccessful efforts to correct the ga
During this period, the truck overturned on one occasion, and
ing the damage from overturning cost the plaintiff nearly $5,50
paying a bit more than half of the purchase price of about
plaintiff declined to make further payments. The dealer rep(
and sold the truck for more than the remainder of the purchas
Plaintiff brought a threefold claim (1) for damage to the trucl
overturning, (2) for return of the payments made on the p
price, and (3) for the loss of business profits in his trucking l
suffered because he was unable to make normal use of the truck

The trial judge found against plaintiff as to damage to the tr

[31] 63 Cal. 2d 9, 403 P.2d 145, 45 Cal. Rptr. 17 (1965).

tained in the accident, because plaintiff failed to show that the defect
—the gallop—caused the accident. He awarded judgment to the plaintiff on the other two elements of the claim. Justice Roger Traynor, writing for the majority, affirmed on the ground that the elements of damages for which recovery was allowed were appropriately awarded for
breach of an express warranty of freedom from defects of material and
workmanship. The disclaimer of liability beyond "making good at its
factory any part or parts thereof" did not defeat liability in this case,
since the warrantor had repeatedly failed "to correct the defect as
promised" and was therefore liable for breach of the promise to do so.
This theory of avoiding a disclaimer would often run into an obstacle
in commonly used provisions declaring that the purchaser must return
the defective part to the factory. Such a contention might be answered
in a situation like that in *Seely*, however, with a theory of estoppel
based on participation of the manufacturers' representatives in the
dealer's efforts to correct the galloping defect.

The majority opinion in *Seely* proceeded to discuss the theory of
strict products liability, indicating that under this theory they would on
proper proof allow damages for accidental physical harm to person or
property, including the product itself, but not for nonphysical economic losses such as were involved in the second and third aspects of
Seely's claim. These nonphysical economic losses, they said, would be
governed by the law of express and implied warranty, including the
UCC. The majority opinion specifically disapproved the New Jersey
court's application of a strict tort liability theory, independent of the
UCC, in the *Santor* case, discussed below.

The concurring-dissenting opinion of Justice Raymond Peters in
Seely argues, on the other hand, that the area governed by the UCC is
marked off by a test concerned with the nature of the transaction. This
opinion would apply the code to claims based on "commercial transactions," but would not classify as "commercial" a purchase by "an ordinary consumer at the end of the marketing chain." Though the question was a close one in Justice Peters' view, he concluded that this
plaintiff, an owner-driver rather than a fleet owner purchasing trucks
regularly in the course of his business, was an ordinary consumer even
though he bought the truck for use in his business. Thus, according to
Justice Peters, the strict products liability theory supports recovery for
nonphysical economic loss as well as physical loss, but in both cases ap-

plies only to noncommercial transactions whereas the UCC applies only to commercial transactions.

The majority opinion in *Seely*, it would seem, distinguishes between, on the one hand, loss within the first three of the eight categories identified above and, on the other hand, loss within the fourth through the eighth. The first three categories concern accidental injuries—to person, to other property, and to the product itself. They concern consequences of unintended happenings that are sudden in the sense that a particular moment in time can be identified as the moment of occurrence. This view seems consistent with the cautiously restrictive position adopted by the American Law Institute in defining the scope of the new strict products liability as depending on "unreasonably dangerous" qualities of the product; [32] this requisite implies that the theory is limited to harms caused by accidents. The remaining five categories involve, on the other hand, if any change at all from a condition existing at the time of transfer, a gradual development rather than sudden occurrence.

Santor [33] presented just such a circumstance of gradual development. The carpet that was supposed to be of even quality with respect to resistance to wear developed streaks as the carpet was used. The New Jersey court allowed the purchaser to recover, on a theory of strict products liability, the difference between the value of a carpet such as this was represented to be and a carpet such as it actually was. The effect of this strict liability rule upon the old law of implied warranty, Justice Peters notes with approval in his concurring-dissenting opinion in *Seely*, is to "abolish the notice requirement, restrict the effectiveness of disclaimers to situations where it can be reasonably said that the consumer has freely assumed the risk, and abolish the privity requirement, where ordinary consumers are involved," rather than to introduce any notion of "defective" different in meaning from "unmerchantable" in the law of implied warranty.

These differing views seem in common to interpret the UCC as inapplicable to whatever area is covered by strict products liability, and thus to treat strict products liability as a theory distinct from express and implied warranty, to which they would hold the code provisions

[32] *Restatement (Second), Torts,* § 402A (1965).
[33] Santor v. A & M Karagheusian, Inc., 44 N.J. 52, 207 A.2d 305 (1965), 16 A.L.R.3d 670 (1967).

applicable. This way of speaking can make for trouble. For example, remedies under express and implied warranty theories have long been granted for injuries caused by impure foods. But it would make no sense to hold that claims for these injuries are governed by the UCC, with the consequence that the plaintiff is disadvantaged by provisions concerning effective notice, privity, and disclaimer, while at the same time holding that one is free of such disadvantages if he is claiming for injuries caused by a defective steering mechanism in an automobile. Traditionally the impure food claims have been more highly favored. To keep them from being even less favored, then, it is necessary to transfer these cases out of the domain of implied warranty and into the domain of strict products liability—if one insists on maintaining separate theories and separate domains for each. Almost as troublesome, too, would be insistence on enforcing procedural niceties of two separate theories of overlapping domains—that is, holding that the plaintiff would lose (for lack of satisfying the notice requirement, for example) if he claimed on implied warranty though he could win if he claimed either solely or alternatively on the strict products liability theory.

Treating strict products liability and implied warranty as two independent theories poses another difficulty. This way of thinking makes it sometimes decisive of results to determine whether the measure of damages under strict products liability doctrine extends to any or all of the last five of the eight categories of claims stated above, rather than merely claims for accidental physical harm to person or property (the first three categories). Of course the substantive issues concerning requisites for recovery upon claims within the last five categories must be faced under any system of doctrine and terminology. But there is risk that these issues will be determined coincidentally rather than by direct examination of their merits if the answers are expressed as a determination that strict products liability does extend to one or more of these categories, or that it does not.

Preferences of courts for one or another terminology should not govern their response to all the underlying substantive questions, including those of statutory interpretation, presented by the various categories of claims for harms and losses caused by products. It would seem that interpreting the UCC provisions as generally inapplicable to claims within the first three categories is fully justified. That is, it seems reasonable to hold that courts are free to abandon the requirement of negligence for all cases in these categories, without invoking the dis-

124

claimer provisions of the UCC that arguably they would be obliged to continue to apply to products-for-human-consumption cases if those cases were to remain, as when the UCC was being developed, under a rubric of exceptionally favorable treatment. To this observer, at least, it would seem also that claims within the fourth through eighth categories are more closely associated with the problems to which the UCC was directed and that courts should feel less free in relation to these types of claims to hold inapplicable the restrictive provisions of the UCC.

Chapter 8

Harms from Traffic Accidents

*T*HE BASIC elements of both the law and the insurance arrangements currently applied to claims arising from traffic accidents came into being before the automobile was invented.

The applicable law is the law of negligence. Rooted in antiquity, it came to full flower in the nineteenth century.

The principal insurance applying to these claims is liability insurance. Invented barely before the automobile, this form of insurance was initially designed to meet the needs of employers for protection against the risk of economic ruin from liabilities to employees in a burgeoning industrial era. It was soon adapted to meet the needs of automobile owners for protection against the risk of economic ruin from liabilities to victims of automobile accidents.

Liability insurance had barely become established when a metamorphosis began. It gradually became an instrument for protecting victims —at first, only in the narrow sense of protecting against the risk of financial irresponsibility of tortfeasors and later in a broader sense of serving a social need for compensating accident victims.

Brief though it is, this sketch of their origins makes the point that the law and insurance arrangements applied to claims of traffic victims as the nation entered the last third of the twentieth century were not the fulfillment of a carefully considered design. The system, if deserving to be called a system, just grew.

Perhaps it is true that institutions that grow with needs tend to have a degree of practicality and utility about them that is difficult to match in any plan. It is also true that this way of development sometimes produces a set of arrangements full of contradictions and waste. This accurately describes the common law system for compensating traffic victims, based on negligence law and liability insurance.

The shortcomings of this system have been detailed elsewhere, along with a proposed reform—the Basic Protection plan.[1] The purpose here

[1] The Basic Protection plan was developed in collaboration with Jeffrey O'Connell of the University of Illinois. We were aided by an excellent research staff and numerous consultants, identified in the preface to Keeton and O'Connell, *Basic Protection for the Traffic Victim—A Blueprint for Reforming Automobile Insurance* (1965). That book presents the Basic Protection proposal in full, in-

is to consider some questions of underlying principle that affect the shaping of any solution to the problems arising from claims of traffic victims.

THE THEORY OF THE FAULT SYSTEM

If we put aside all the liability insurance aspects of the fault system and examine only the tort law of automobile accident cases, we find a system dominated by the principle of basing liability on negligence. In general, it is the theory of the system that a victim should bear his own loss if it resulted from an accident in which nobody was negligent, or if he alone was negligent, or if both he and another were negligent. Conversely, by this theory he should recover compensation for his losses, and for pain and suffering as well, if he was innocent and someone else was negligent in causing the accident. As will be seen in Chapter 9, attempts to justify this principle on grounds concerned with punishment and deterrence are unpersuasive. In final analysis the weightiest argument for the principle is a candid appeal to fairness—an assertion that most people believe it is fair to make wrongdoers bear the burden of accidental losses they cause and unfair to impose on innocent persons any burden of losses caused by wrongdoers.

If the range of possible solutions were limited to placing the burden of a particular loss on an innocent party or a wrongdoer, it would be hard indeed to find any sensible ground for challenging the fault principle. Consciously or subconsciously, proponents of the fault principle have commonly sought to win the day by limiting the field of battle in this way.

If we extend our analysis of the system to its liability insurance aspects as well as the tort doctrine, we quickly discover that there is in fact an escape from the narrow choice of making either a plaintiff or a defendant bear the burden of traffic accident loss.

In the first place, when liability within insurance coverage is established the loss is borne not by the plaintiff, not by the defendant, and

---

cluding a draft statute and comments upon it section by section. The proposal is presented in less detail in Keeton and O'Connell, *After Cars Crash—The Need for Legal and Insurance Reform* (1967). Additions to the proposal, including provisions for covering damage to automobiles as well as personal injuries, are presented in the proceedings of a conference at Champaign, Illinois, in October 1967, *Crisis in Car Insurance*, pp. 69–79 (Keeton, O'Connell, and McCord, eds., 1968). An optional version of the proposal, developed in 1968, can be found in Massachusetts House Bill 4820, which passed the House of Representatives but failed in the Senate in that year.

from a long-range point of view not even by the insurance company, but by the thousands who have paid insurance premiums. Observe what this does to the fundamental premise of the common law system that wrongdoers shall bear the burden. The one person classified as a wrongdoer by the common law has paid only a very tiny fraction of the accumulation of premiums out of which this judgment is paid. All the remainder of the premiums were paid by persons at least as innocent of any wrongdoing in relation to this accident as the most innocent victim could be, and no doubt more innocent than most victims. Moreover, all but a small percentage of these premium payers will have had no connection with *any* accident during the entire period of policy coverage for which their premiums were paid. Thus, liability insurance converts the common law system from a system for imposing losses on wrongdoers to a system for distributing losses through insurance to a large group of persons most of whom are innocent of any wrongdoing not only from the perspective of a case under adjudication but also from the perspective of the total body of cases for a premium period.

It may be suggested in response that a principle of imposing burdens on wrongdoers can still be maintained under liability insurance by adjusting rates to driving records. But as long as the insurance principle is used, only a small fraction of the burden is shifted to the wrongdoers through higher rates in succeeding years, and this means that other premium payers must make up the difference. If the amount recovered from each individual wrongdoer in future premiums were actually sufficient to cover the loss he caused, the system would cease to be one of genuine insurance and would become instead essentially a lending system under which in effect the wrongdoer had to pay back over time the funds used to discharge a liability to the victim on his behalf. No system of merit rating—that is, adjusting premiums to accident records —has ever been pushed this far. Rather, merit rating systems operate on a basis that is crude indeed as judged by the criterion of responsibility for exact repayment of the loss by the tortfeasor. The increase of premiums charged to a driver responsible for an accident from which relatively little loss occurs may be many times greater than the loss, and the increase charged to one responsible for an accident giving rise to a very large tort judgment, however long the increased charges are paid, invariably totals less than the amount of the judgment.

Liability insurance, then, converts the claims system to one that distributes losses. In the process, it also allocates the burden on a very different basis from that implicit in the fault principle of the underlying tort law, upon which the liability insurance is superimposed.

SOME PRAGMATIC SHORTCOMINGS OF THE FAULT SYSTEM

There is a fundamental pragmatic question about the efficacy of the fault principle for automobile accident litigation. Is it an impractical criterion of liability, however appealing it might otherwise be in theory? The pragmatic difficulties include the deterioration of evidence between the time of the accident and a long delayed trial, the paucity of competent observers of the crucial event, and the extra burdens that split-second time sequences place on the capacity of witnesses to perceive, recall, and narrate. "These difficulties cumulate, we are told, so that the actual trial almost necessarily involves an imperfect and ambiguous historical reconstruction of the event, making a mockery of the effort to apply so subtle a normative criterion to the conduct involved. An impenetrable evidentiary screen thus makes fault unworkable as a criterion whatever its merits as a concept." [2]

This crisp and eloquent summary of the pragmatic criticisms is the work of Walter J. Blum and Harry Kalven, Jr., the most noted academic champions of the fault principle. It sets the stage for their response:

> But does not this objection run the risk of proving too much? All adjudication is vulnerable to the inadequacies of evidence and the consequent exploitation of the situation by the skill of counsel. From prosecutions for murder to adjudications of the validity of family partnership for income tax purposes, the law has had to wrestle with these difficulties. Auto accidents are at least more public than many other legal situations and they almost invariably do leave physical traces. The witness to an auto accident is asked for observations likely to be well within his daily experience. The law can tolerate a goodly margin of error, and the threshold of distortion which this line of attack on liability for fault must establish before it becomes a persuasive reason for throwing over the system is high. We remain skeptical that the evidentiary aspects of the auto accident are so peculiar as to be set apart from the evidentiary aspects of all other controversies that are brought to law.[3]

[2] Walter J. Blum and Harry Kalven, Jr., *Public Law Perspectives on a Private Law Problem—Auto Compensation Plans* (1965), p. 9. This study was published earlier as an article, 31 *U. Chi. L. Rev.* 641, 647 (1964).
[3] *Ibid.*, pp. 9–10 (31 *U. Chi. L. Rev.*, pp. 647–648).

On this question Blum and Kalven plainly represent a minority point of view among academicians. Certainly the comments of Dean William L. Prosser, for example, are not to be discounted as the exaggerations of an overzealous reformer. His writings as a whole display a detached skepticism toward proposals for reform in this area. Yet, this is his assessment of litigation in automobile accident cases:

> The process by which the question of legal fault, and hence of liability, is determined in our courts is a cumbersome, time-consuming, expensive, and almost ridiculously inaccurate one. The evidence given in personal injury cases usually consists of highly contradictory statements from the two sides, estimating such factors as time, speed, distance and visibility, offered months after the event by witnesses who were never very sure just what happened when they saw it, and whose faulty memories are undermined by lapse of time, by bias, by conversations with others, and by the subtle influence of counsel. Upon such evidence, a jury of twelve inexperienced citizens, called away from their other business if they have any, are invited to retire and make the best guess they can as to whether the defendant, the plaintiff, or both were "negligent," which is itself a wobbly and uncertain standard based upon the supposed mental processes of a hypothetical and non-existent reasonable man. European lawyers view the whole thing with utter amazement; and the extent to which it has damaged the courts and the legal profession by bringing the law and its administration into public disrepute can only be guessed.[4]

Among trial lawyers, no doubt the weight of opinion is the reverse of that among academicians. But now and then a trial lawyer, too, is heard to exclaim about the unrealistic quality of automobile accident litigation.[5]

It may be that to some extent the partisans of these contrasting points of view are talking about different things. One who focuses his attention upon the accuracy and reliability of a reconstruction, months or years later, of the relative movements of vehicles during a two-second time interval—movements upon which right-of-way at an intersection may turn—sees the process as more fanciful than realistic, more

[4] Prosser, *Torts* (3rd ed. 1964), § 85, p. 580.
[5] See the comments of Laurence H. Eldredge of the Philadelphia bar, reproduced in Keeton and O'Connell, *Basic Protection for the Traffic Victim,* pp. 19–20.

a product of imaginative afterthought than a faithful description of historical events. On the other hand, one who focuses his attention on the relative blameworthiness of the parties to an accident in which a drunken driver runs through a stop sign and strikes a pedestrian in a crosswalk sees the assessment of blame as not only realistic but so compelling that it would be outrageous to disregard it. There are some cases in which fault can be assessed realistically, and other cases in which this is not true.

In part, then, the problem is not that fault is inherently an unworkable criterion for all cases but that the particular criterion of fault we have evolved in automobile cases is unworkable for a high percentage of these cases.

Liability insurance is partly responsible for the distinctive evolution of this fault concept. If tort law were functioning during the automobile age without the superstructure of insurance, arguably it would be possible to maintain standards for determining negligence that would tend more nearly to cull out the cases in which blame can be assessed realistically and to limit findings of negligence to that group. Once liability insurance had been conceived, however, this was no longer possible. The pressures for using this mechanism to extend compensation to a far greater percentage of victims than could have been successful in their claims under a rigorous fault criterion were irresistible. Moreover, these pressures would undoubtedly have required the invention of liability insurance, or some alternative, had it not already entered the scene before the automobile.

The prospect of returning to realistic criteria of fault cannot be taken seriously as long as a tort and liability insurance system is expected to serve as the major source of compensation for traffic victims. If another kind of system is assigned the primary role of compensating those injured in traffic accidents, however, genuine assessments of fault could play an important part in allocating both benefits and burdens.

Unhappily, the cases tried under the fault system tend to be those in which application of the fault criterion is most unrealistic. Cases in which the criterion can be realistically applied tend to be settled, unless there are intractable disputes concerning the amount of damage, and even then the trial focuses more upon the damages issues than upon a dispute about whether there was fault. The fault issue is emphasized, if at all, as a technique for affecting the damages finding. On the other hand, cases in which the fault criterion is less realistic are more debatable, more difficult to settle, and thus more often within the small percentage of cases that actually reach trial. Thus, the system inherently tends to select for trial a disproportionately high number of the cases that most dramatically demonstrate the system's deficiencies. Since it also happens, at least among the cases reaching lawyers, that the percentage in which the fault criterion is unrealistic probably exceeds the percentage in which it is realistic, the lay observer's assessment of the automobile accident litigation he sees in courts is not likely to be generous to lawyers and the law.

At the very least, then, it appears that the fault criterion is unsatisfactory for a large percentage of the total volume of claims and an even larger percentage of the relatively few claims that the system selects for trial.

FAIR ALLOCATION OF LOSSES

The fault criterion, found wanting on pragmatic grounds, is even less satisfactory from the point of view of fair allocation of responsibility for all of the damages resulting from automobile accidents—including both economic loss and pain and suffering.

Perhaps this point can be seen most clearly by comparing accident experience in circumstances alike except for density of traffic and other changes that increased traffic brings. For example, suppose a ten-mile stretch of rural two-lane highway, where a substantial percentage of motorists drive ten miles per hour faster than the speed limit. One may argue about whether this conduct is genuinely blameworthy, but at least in the absence of a limited number of recognized excuses, it is negligence. It may happen that relatively few of these drivers are called to account for their conduct because the road is not heavily traveled and there are relatively few accidents.

Now suppose a business boom in the area. Traffic congestion results, lower speed limits are posted, and a high percentage of drivers continue to operate at speeds a little above the limit. The accident frequency goes up, not merely in proportion to the increase in traffic but more. In time, a parallel toll road is constructed. This only partly relieves the congestion of the older road, and the frequency of accidents continues higher than it was in the good old days when the road was sparsely used.

Negligence law decrees that ordinarily when two of the slightly

132

speeding drivers on this congested road collide each is to bear his own loss. All the other speeding drivers, and the nonspeeding users of the road as well, contribute nothing to meeting the burden of these losses. Thus each driver on this highway who is committing essentially the same offense as the slightly speeding drivers of the good old days is subject to a much greater risk of suffering serious consequences. But it is only a risk. Some of the slightly speeding drivers pay the penalty and others do not. Negligence law treats the consequences of an accident in each of these settings as totally the responsibility of the parties to that accident. It treats the increased level of losses suffered by persons using this road under the new circumstances as totally the responsibility of the unlucky minority who happen to be involved in the accidents, while allowing the lucky majority to use the road without contributing anything to the cost of paying for these accidents. This holds true even in the face of the clear demonstration, by the proximity of the toll road and its better safety record, that most of the accidents could be avoided by charging all users enough to pay for a better road.

One point made by this comparison is that even the innocent users of our congested highways are contributing to the circumstances that breed a predictable toll of accidents. They are realizing a saving in using the less expensive roadway rather than paying through taxes or tolls to support the construction of safer roads that would reduce the accident toll. Even if the conduct of the drivers in a particular accident is such that we can genuinely classify it as blameworthy, and thus deserving of being burdened with a greater share of the losses resulting, their blameworthy conduct is not the sole cause of the accidents. The traffic congestion on the poor road contributes too. Part of the burden of compensating for the loss, then, should be borne by others who contribute to the congestion but happen to be lucky enough not to be in a collision.

Taking into account the fact that losses may be distributed, rather than merely being shifted, broadens one's perspective. From this broader perspective, often it does not seem fair that either of the two drivers should bear the burden the law assigns him. For example, if the accident is unavoidable in the legal sense—that is, it happened without negligence—it may be that traffic congestion and a poor road were contributing factors. Under these circumstances, many other persons are benefiting equally with the two victims of the accident in gaining the advantage of travel on the highway and avoiding the expense of higher taxes for improvement of the roads. It seems grossly unfair to impose this burden of accidental losses on a few who happen to be involved in accidents rather than to distribute it widely among the beneficiaries of greater travel and lower taxes. Moreover, a practical mechanism is available for accomplishing distribution: automobile insurance.

Consider another example too. Who would count as a work of justice the denial of compensation to the innocent pedestrian who, while walking along a sidewalk, is struck by a car that jumps the curb out of control because its driver, with no previous history of heart disease, suffers an unpredictable heart attack?

Nor does it seem fair that the *whole* cost of even those accidents in which one or more drivers were at fault should be borne by those drivers. The quality of the road and the volume of traffic can be contributing factors even to these accidents.

Liability insurance has sharply reduced the pressure that might otherwise have existed for openly recognizing that traffic congestion and poor roads contribute to the accident toll, and for causing part of the cost to be allocated accordingly. Though designed on a different theory, it actually serves the function of allocating losses widely among the whole group of motorists who obtain liability insurance. The practice has been wiser and fairer than the theory.

Even as ameliorated by liability insurance, however, the common law system of negligence liability is grossly unfair in its allocation of both benefits and burdens.

In practice it unfairly allocates the total fund of benefits it administers by making generous and even profligate awards in some cases while awarding little or nothing in others, all under the banner of criteria that themselves condemn the actual distribution as unfair. Under its theory, the victim is supposed to receive all (including reasonable compensation for pain and suffering) or nothing. In practice, however, relatively few victims receive nothing, virtually all severely injured persons receive far less than even their out-of-pocket loss, and many persons with very minor injuries, resulting in very little loss, are heavily overpaid because of the nuisance value of virtually any claim of a twinge in the back, whether real or imaginary.

The fault system also unfairly allocates the burden of providing funds for compensation since it fails to take due account of the principle that motoring should pay its way in the sense of having part of the highway toll treated as a share to be distributed among motorists generally.

It is suggested in Chapter 9 that activities generally should pay their way in society by shouldering the burden of the distinctive risks they cause. The application of this broad principle to traffic cases supports the idea that at least part of the cost of accidents should be distributed among motorists generally. Community choices about the numbers of vehicles and kinds of drivers allowed and about the cost and quality of roads affect the accident toll and ought to be taken into account in allocating the burden of paying for these losses.

Partisans of the fault system respond that paying non-fault insurance benefits would "reward wrongdoers" and that this would be less equitable than a system of negligence law and liability insurance. In thus defending liability insurance while attacking non-fault benefits as rewards to wrongdoers they engage in a curious self-contradiction. By its own theory, liability insurance is the one form of insurance that is designed to protect nobody but wrongdoers. It pays only on their behalf, and only because they have been guilty of wrongs. It has survived because, regardless of this theory, it has come to be used not merely for protecting wrongdoers but for helping the victims as well. In financial responsibility legislation enacted in every state, this latter objective has been legitimated at least as to assuring that the victim will have some financially responsible defendant to sue.

The next natural step is to make primary the objective of helping victims. One can wisely choose still to adhere to this objective even if it sometimes happens incidentally that losses suffered by wrongdoers are reimbursed. Also, one can do this and still avoid allowing either to wrongdoers or to victims, whether at fault or not, real profits such as the present system allows (for example, by permitting overlapping benefits and by encouraging nuisance settlements for claims of pain and suffering damages based on negligence).

It is relevant too that liability insurance protects a wrongdoer from the economic consequences of his wrong with a fund collected from people even more clearly innocent than the innocent victim. If supporters of the fault system do not consider this "rewarding" wrongdoers, then a fortiori they should acknowledge that insurance under which a policyholder collects from his company, to which he has paid the premium for his protection, does not "reward" wrongdoing or wrongdoers merely because it reimburses losses regardless of fault.

To whatever extent provisions for compensation fall short of assuring every victim *full* compensation at least for out-of-pocket loss, the system fails to assure distribution of loss—that is, it fails to spread it among a large group and instead leaves it to be borne by an individual. To this extent, the system must still confront the argument that as between just two individuals—an innocent victim and a blameworthy driver—it seems unfair to make the victim bear the loss. To escape this argument and its basic appeal to one's sense of what is fair, a pure non-fault system must come at least very close to compensating fully for all out-of-pocket loss. But no non-fault system has yet offered that much to victims. The reason, it would seem, is cost. Thus, a pure non-fault system that pays full compensation costs too much, and one that falls far short of full compensation at least for out-of-pocket losses is too inequitable.

It may seem, from another perspective, that this cost-equity dilemma is illusory. It may be said, for example, that the overall cost of a system of full compensation (including payments not only for out-of-pocket loss but also for pain and suffering) would not be substantially greater, if greater at all, than the costs of the fault system or any other. Traffic accidents produce a toll of loss and misery whether compensation is paid or not. The fault system decrees that innocent victims pay a substantial share of this toll. Changing that decree to transfer part of this burden to others does not increase the overall burden except to the extent of the cost of administering the transfer. And that cost is somewhat offset by savings, because a system in which the transfer is accomplished by means that avoid crushing individual burdens reduces secondary losses resulting from inability of some individuals to bear these assigned burdens.

Instructive as this perspective may be, it does not eliminate the pragmatic cost-equity dilemma. It may suggest that a wise society should be able to find a way of financing full compensation, but the practical problem of finding a politically acceptable method of financing remains.

Even if the problem of financing could be solved somehow, there is another perspective from which a non-fault system of full reimbursement of losses might be inequitable. Equity is needed not only in the distribution of payments but also in the distribution of the burden of financing these payments.

It may be argued that it is not essential to the equity of a non-fault system that it extend to full reimbursement of out-of-pocket losses. It may be said, for example, that some people because of their high earned incomes represent high risks to the system, and that it would be inequitable to make those with lower incomes subsidize this group. To avoid such a subsidy, a non-fault insurance system that pays full reimbursement might charge much higher insurance premiums to the high earners. But this is not the only way to achieve equity. Another way is to place moderate limits on the level of reimbursement—including a limit for wage losses suffered during any given period of time—and set the high earner's premiums consistently with the system's limit on benefits, leaving him free to make additional provisions, by added insurance or otherwise, for protection against the excess of his risk over this moderate limit. Still we must face the question whether this is fair to the innocent, high-earning victims of blameworthy drivers. It seems likely that most people would think not. This is not to say that their judgment is indisputably correct, but only to suggest that it exists and constitutes a political force relevant to the cost-equity dilemma.

It may be suggested that people can and do accept a result somewhat like this, growing out of the financial irresponsibility of blameworthy drivers under the fault system. A high earner with large losses —or, for that matter, even a low earner with long-term losses—seldom recovers in full against a blameworthy but impecunious driver. Full recovery is prevented by his limited financial responsibility and the inadequate amount of his liability insurance coverage, if any. But at least this can be seen as not so much an inequity in the system itself as a misfortune of poverty, the impact of which extends even to those beyond the impoverished group. People can accept bad luck with a certain philosophic resignation not so readily accorded to bad law. Thus, the point remains that a pure non-fault system that does not pay substantially full reimbursement will, standing alone, seem inequitable.

It might be argued that equity requires also that payments for pain and suffering be available when fault is proved if they are not a part of the non-fault coverage. This argument seems less persuasive, however, than the corresponding argument regarding out-of-pocket loss. One reason this is so is that the needs served by payments for pain and suffering are less compelling than those served by compensation for out-of-pocket loss.

Clearly, it is ordinarily more difficult to determine how much pain and suffering has occurred than to determine out-of-pocket loss. It is likewise more difficult to place a dollar value on pain. These problems of administration produce a significant increase in the overhead cost of a system when it attempts to compensate for pain and suffering. In cases of minor injury, the overhead cost of pruning away exaggeration and of valuing genuine pain and suffering may even exceed the amount of fair compensation. Thus it may be said that it is both more prudent and more equitable to apply the available resources to the more compelling need—compensating for out-of-pocket losses as far as possible—than to use resources in an inefficient effort to compensate for pain and suffering associated with injuries that are not severe.

This point loses force, however, as the injury and the pain and suffering associated with it grow more serious. For example, consider severe disfigurement of a type that plastic surgery cannot overcome. Although there will be disputes about the severity of the mental distress and about how many dollars should be paid in compensation, the overhead cost of resolving them may be modest in relation to the amount required for fair compensation. In relation to injuries of this severity, perhaps the argument that equity requires compensation for pain and suffering approaches the force of the argument for reimbursing out-of-pocket losses. Arguably, then, the cost side of the cost-equity dilemma concerns not only out-of-pocket losses but also pain and suffering in cases of severe injury, even though a different view may be taken of claims to compensation for pain and suffering associated with lesser injuries.

If it were feasible to assure unlimited financial responsibility for payments, it might well seem best to capitalize upon the greater efficiency of a non-fault system of compensation and wholly eliminate tort actions for compensation. This could be done either with or without the use of fault as a criterion for bearing shares of the burden of financing, through a merit rating system for pricing insurance, or otherwise. If limits are placed on the extent to which a system compensates for losses regardless of fault, and for pain as well in cases of severe injury, the argument for allowing claims based on fault for losses above those limits becomes more cogent. Perhaps it is no mere accident of history that in countries having systems of reparation through social security or private non-fault insurance—invariably limited—some system for asserting liability for losses above those limits is also maintained.[6] It would seem, then, that the most promising possibility for a reasonably

[6] See Keeton and O'Connell, *Basic Protection for the Traffic Victim*, pp. 189–219.

satisfactory resolution of the cost-equity dilemma is a blended system that pays regardless of fault for the out-of-pocket losses of all victims up to a moderate limit—thus holding costs within reasonable bounds —and provides that when an innocent victim is injured by truly blameworthy driving, he may obtain compensation based on fault for losses above this basic level, and for pain and suffering as well in cases of severe injury.

WHAT TYPE REFORM?

Reform of the system for compensating traffic victims seems a certainty. The most significant question to be resolved is what the fundamental character of the new system will be.

Perhaps the most drastic change proposed in any quarter is the suggestion that the entire tort system of compensating for personal injuries be abandoned in favor of a social security system. The New Zealand Commission on Compensation, reporting in December 1967, advanced such a proposal. Their report takes note that this would mean supplanting private insurance for personal injury compensation, including workmen's compensation, since there would no longer be any need to determine whether an injury giving rise to a claim occurred at work or at play, in the factory, in the automobile, or at home.[7] In the United States, too, some observers are urging at least a far greater use of the social security mechanism, if not such comprehensive use as the New Zealand commission proposes.[8] And in 1968 Puerto Rico enacted a sys-

[7] Royal Commission of Inquiry, Report, Compensation for Personal Injury in New Zealand (1967), pp. 20–21, 24–26.

[8] See, for example, Franklin, "Replacing the Negligence Lottery: Compensation and Selective Reimbursement," 53 *Va. L. Rev.* 774 (1967); Conard, "The Economic Treatment of Automobile Injuries," 63 *Mich. L. Rev.* 279 (1964). Blum and Kalven, though defending the fault system, seem also to express a preference for social security over any intermediate solution; see their *Public Law Perspectives on a Private Law Problem*, pp. 83–85 (31 *U. Chi. L. Rev.* 641, 721–723). See also Moynihan, "Next: A New Auto Insurance Policy," New York *Times Magazine*, Aug. 27, 1967, p. 26. Moynihan's article has sometimes been interpreted as proposing a government system of automobile insurance, but it seems a more reasonable reading of his article that he poses such a system merely as the only viable alternative to a fundamental reform of private insurance, such as the Basic Protection plan. For example, he says: "Variations on the Keeton-O'Connell proposal are certainly possible . . . But in all its essentials, it is hard to deny the fundamental rightness of the Basic Protection plan" (p. 82). "What is to be done? The first and obvious step is the opening of Congressional hearings . . . But the essential step is for the leaders of the insurance industry itself to take on the issue—directly, openly, willingly. Is this out of the question? Some small part of the future of American private enterprise will be determined by the response to that possibility" (p. 83).

tem that relies heavily on social security, though retaining tort claims and private insurance for compensation above the social security benefits.[9]

Another proposal is that responsibility for this whole problem be shifted from the states to the federal government by the adoption of a national compensation plan for automobile victims, patterned after workmen's compensation.[10]

Both social security and workmen's compensation solutions are open to criticism because experience demonstrates that the benefits would be well below losses. Moreover, the leveling effect of scheduled benefits, common in social security and workmen's compensation systems, produces arbitrariness as well as inadequacy. This criticism has maximum cogency against a system with the low and inflexible schedules of social security. It has great force, still, against the somewhat less pared and rigid schedules of workmen's compensation. Its force would increase if such schedules were applied to the more diverse group of victims who must be compensated for traffic injuries. Their work, their income, and the many factors bearing on their losses would be far less alike than is the case among the employees of a given industry, covered by a common schedule of workmen's compensation benefits. Nor is it an answer to this criticism that, in contrast with workmen's compensation, social security systems have already been extended to this more diverse group. Social security has been used to provide subsistence-level benefits, or perhaps a little better, and never to compensate fully on a basis concerned with what is equitable in light of the greater losses suffered by some.

Rather than adopting these more drastic and less equitable solutions, it would seem wiser to tailor a reform to distinctive problems and needs.

In the assessment of unfairness of the fault system, very small claims figure prominently. They are the claims that so often produce overpayment, largely as a result of nuisance value. They are the source of other ills as well. It is with respect to the small claims that the wastefulness of the fault system is most apparent. The costs of investigation and preparation for controversies over fault and over the valuation of

[9] The Puerto Rican plan is described by its authors, Juan Aponte and Herbert Denenberg, in "The Automobile Problem in Puerto Rico: Dimensions and Proposed Solution," 35 *J. Risk and Ins.* 227 (1968); "An Addendum," *ibid.*, p. 637.
[10] See, for example, Hofstadter and Pesner, "A National Compensation Plan for Automobile Accident Cases," 22 *Record of N.Y.C. Bar Ass'n* 615 (1967).

pain and suffering in the multitude of small and medium-sized negligence claims are greatly disproportionate to the amounts at issue. In the low percentage of these claims that actually reach trial, the total costs for preparing and litigating far outstrip the amount of compensation awarded, even when the claimant is successful.

The importance of dealing with this central problem of the small and medium-sized negligence claims is driven home by data concerning their number. It has been reported, for example, that in 1962, of all bodily injury claims paid by liability insurance companies on passenger car coverage, approximately 89 percent were paid in amounts less than $2000 per case, 79 percent in amounts less than $1000, and 62 percent in amounts less than $500.[11] Field studies indicate that in most instances of settlement under $500, the loss was less than $100, and often the net loss was still less because the bills were already covered—and sometimes covered twice or more—by other kinds of insurance.[12]

Defenders of the fault system argue that these payments above and beyond loss are based on fault and are paid for pain and suffering. But a liability insurance company can and usually does make a settlement with the other person even when its policyholder thinks he was not at fault, because it costs far more to defend against a small claim than to pay it.

Small claims are the worst offenders, then, as to both the inequity of overpayment and the wastefulness of the system. It also happens that these are the claims that can be paid on a non-fault basis, limited to out-of-pocket loss, with the least stress under the cost-equity dilemma. The greatest hope for effective reform of the fault system lies in changing the way claims for less than severe injury are treated. This can be done, too, consistently with the principle that motoring should pay its way.

From a broad perspective, three sets of principles compete for dominance in systems for compensating traffic victims: principles of fault (supplemented with liability insurance), loss insurance (paying for accidental losses regardless of who was at fault), and social security.

The first of these has been dominant in the United States. The second has come into increasing prominence with the wide use of collision

---

[11] Calculated from data provided by Frank Harwayne, F.C.A.S., an independent consulting actuary of New York City.
[12] See generally Keeton and O'Connell, *Basic Protection for the Traffic Victim*, pp. 34–69.

insurance (paying for damage to cars regardless of who was at fault) and medical payments insurance (paying hospital and medical bills regardless of fault). Thus far, at least, the social security principle has been little used for covering traffic losses.

Perhaps the main arguments advanced in the controversy over these principles are concerned with equity and cost. A system founded on fault and liability insurance is sharply criticized on both these counts, and valiantly defended on the ground that its higher costs are a reasonable price to pay for the greater equity its supporters see in such a system. A system giving dominance to loss insurance is supported with claims of lower costs and greater equity. It is attacked from both sides —by partisans of liability insurance primarily on the ground that it is inequitable under their standards, and by partisans of social security primarily on the ground that its overhead costs are too great. Indeed, although those advocating the social security principle argue that their system would produce equity by their standard, perhaps the argument they most emphasize is that it would sharply reduce overhead.

Certainly a social security system could avoid much of the overhead inherent in liability insurance and to a lesser extent in loss insurance. It need not incur the costs of determining who was at fault in an accident, or the costs of allocating burdens in relation to contributions to motoring risks, or the costs of allocating levels of benefits so they are closely related to actual losses suffered by individual victims. A social security system is more efficient, then, because it is more standardized. From a less friendly perspective, it may be said that it is more efficient because it is more arbitrary—less concerned about fairness among all the persons who receive its benefits and bear the burden of paying its costs.

If a social security system is modified to give more attention to equity, its overhead goes up. For example, if maximum benefits are raised from a bare subsistence level to a level approaching the actual losses suffered by most victims, overhead is significantly increased in two ways. First, it costs more to determine actual losses case by case than to use a subsistence standard of benefits in all cases. Second, it costs more to protect against fraudulent or exaggerated claims when benefits for claimed inability to work approach what the claimant could receive by returning to work.

A major policy question to be faced, then, is whether the added overhead cost is a reasonable price to pay for fairer distribution of the burdens and benefits of the system.

Loss insurance, it is submitted, should be the major source of compensation for traffic victims, and especially for losses resulting from the multitude of small and medium-sized cases in which the costs of a liability insurance system are heavily disproportionate to the losses. Though loss insurance inherently has a somewhat greater overhead cost than a social security system, this is a reasonable price to pay for the wiser and fairer distribution of burdens and benefits it achieves. It is a wiser distribution because it enables society generally and decision makers individually to take account of the real costs of motoring when faced with choices about roads and cars. It is a fairer distribution because it helps to place upon those who benefit from motoring that part of the cost of the activity resulting from accidents it produces.

This is not to say that loss insurance should be relied upon exclusively. Rather, to meet the cost-equity dilemma, it seems wise and fair to pay losses up to a moderate limit by loss insurance, eliminating negligence claims within that range, while preserving a fault system as a source of added compensation for the victims of more severe injury.

Such a combined system is in fact less of a departure from tradition than it might seem on its face. Neither in the United States nor elsewhere in the world today is the function of compensating traffic victims assigned exclusively to one alone among the three major sets of principles that compete for dominance. Rather, every system is a blend. In this respect, as we shall see in Chapter 9, the problem of compensating traffic victims is but an illustration of a more pervasive need for wise accommodation of varied interests as the legal system renews itself to meet contemporary problems.

Three

A Perspective on the Future

Chapter 9
Blending Old and New

*C*ONCERN with law reform naturally produces emphasis on the new. At any given time, however, even when the spirit of change is at its peak, all that is new both in substantive law and in legal process appears in perspective as a relatively small part of the total legal system. Any comprehensive view of reform must deal with the problem of blending old and new into a unified system.

In tort law, the bedrock of the old is negligence. The principle of basing awards for accidental injuries on negligence achieved the status of an axiom in Anglo-American tort law some time in the nineteenth century. Vigorous debate over the merits of the negligence principle was soon to follow. At first, such debate was primarily academic. More recently, lawyers and judges have joined the fray, not alone for diversion but as well in responding to immediate concerns. A genuine reassessment of negligence law is occurring. As one route to sharpening appraisal of the role of negligence, and prediction for the future, consider what objectives negligence law is capable of serving and how its performance measures against that of alternative principles.

OBJECTIVES SERVED BY BASING LIABILITY ON NEGLIGENCE

The primary objective of Anglo-American tort law is fair and just compensation for losses. Sometimes it serves the cause of justice to shift a loss from one to another; at other times, to leave it where it has fallen.

The machinery of adjudication will not be set in motion without good reason. Its operation is expensive. From the community point of view, using it to shift a loss is not worth the price unless shifting the loss serves some good purpose. This principle of inertia of the machinery of adjudication serves as a starting point for discussing bases of liability in tort.

Occasionally it is said that the primary function of tort law is compensation of losses. This statement is at best a half-truth. The principle of inertia reminds us that sometimes compensation should not be allowed. Courts should leave a loss where they find it unless good reason for shifting it appears. The mere fact that one member of society is compensated when the court shifts a loss is not such a reason, since the gain is offset by the loss shifted to another member of society.

In general, fault has been the most widely acceptable reason for shifting loss. Particularly in the last half of the nineteenth and the first half of the twentieth centuries, fault occupied the position of the one generally acceptable reason for judicial loss shifting—the principal theme of tort law.

Whether this theme has more ancient lineage is sharply debated, as an illustrative range of opinions will show. W. S. Holdsworth and James Barr Ames take the position that in early common law conduct was judged more by results than by intentions.[1] John Henry Wigmore suggests that law began with an amoral concept that a man acts at his peril, and gradually developed toward a theme of liability based on fault.[2] Percy H. Winfield counters that it has never been true that "a man acts at his peril" if by that phrase it is meant that a man is liable for whatever harm he does to another; even the so-called absolute liability in trespass was subject to grounds of justification and excuse.[3] Oliver Wendell Holmes, Jr., suggests that in early law liability was associated with revenge, that it was based on the thought that someone or something was to blame. Though in a sense law always measures liability by moral standards, he says, it is continually transmuting them into external or objective standards, from which the actual guilt of the party concerned is wholly eliminated.[4] Still another point of view is taken by Nathan Isaacs, who suggests that culpability has always been an important factor in determining rules of liability and that the degree of emphasis on culpability has alternately waxed and waned.[5] Harper and James summarize by saying that a study of common law decisions supports these conclusions:

> (1) the gist of liability in trespass was that defendant's act directly produced the injury; (2) probably the complete absence of any negligence would defeat the action; (3) but if it would, this was matter of defense to be affirmatively pleaded and proved by de-

[1] W. S. Holdsworth, *A History of English Law* (5th ed. 1942), III, 375; Ames, "Law and Morals," 22 *Harv. L. Rev.* 97 (1908).

[2] Wigmore, "Responsibility for Tortious Acts: Its Legal History" (pts. 1–3), 7 *Harv. L. Rev.* 315, 383, 441 (1894).

[3] Winfield, "The Myth of Absolute Liability," 42 *L. Q. Rev.* 37 (1926).

[4] Oliver Wendell Holmes, Jr., *The Common Law* (1881), Lectures 1, 3, 4.

[5] Isaacs, "Fault and Liability," 31 *Harv. L. Rev.* 954 (1918).

fendant; it came in, so to speak, by the back door; (4) the concept of negligence was not dominant enough—at least in this form of action —and not well enough worked out in the mind of the profession so that its opposite was ever successfully formulated as a defense to an action of trespass before the nineteenth century.[6]

The evidence is inconclusive, but perhaps the most appealing inference is that the theme of fault is as ancient as law itself and that early common law conceptions of responsibility for harms one had caused were rustic definitions of fault. The notions of causation and fault are close kin. Picking one or more *responsible causes* from the multitude of antecedents of a given incident is very close to finding fault. This view finds support in Holdsworth's observations, even though he takes the position that during the medieval period (1066–1485) civil liability was not concerned with fault but rather rested on a primitive basis that one is liable for harms caused by his acts. This principle, Holdsworth contends, continued to occupy a major role in civil liability into the nineteenth century. He observes, however, that even in the medieval period, one's liability was limited to the proximate consequences of his acts. This "limitation of liability," he adds, "was perhaps accepted as a measure of obvious justice without a precise analysis of its consequences and bearing upon the prevalent theory of civil liability. The conception of negligence is latent in such a limitation; but in this period this latent consequence has not been discovered." [7]

It may be that to early common law lawyers, and even until the nineteenth century flowering of negligence, there was no such concept as an unavoidable accident in the modern sense of one for which no person is to be blamed.[8] With the exception of a few extraordinary oc-

[6] Harper and James, *Torts* (1956), vol. II, § 12.2, pp. 748–749 (footnotes omitted).

[7] Holdsworth, *A History of English Law*, III, 379–380.

[8] One might so interpret the report of Weaver v. Ward, Hob. 134, 80 Eng. Rep. 284 (K.B. c.1616). Judgment was given the plaintiff upon his demurrer to the defendant's plea that the plaintiff and the defendant were soldiers engaged in training when, by accident, his musket was discharged and plaintiff was wounded. The report states, "and therefore no man shall be excused of a trespass . . . except it may be judged utterly without his fault; as if . . . the defendant had . . . set forth the case with the circumstances, so as it had appeared to the Court that it had been inevitable, and that the defendant had committed no negligence to give occasion to the hurt." It seems a permissible inference from this ambiguous passage that its author thought that an unintended hurt was either *negligently* caused by defendant or *not* caused by defendant; in the latter event, it was "inevitable" and occurred utterly without his fault.

It has been said that this was the first of a line of cases in which "inevitable

currences attributed to the deity, perhaps every accident was thought to be avoidable. It may even be that if ever this idea ceased to be current it has been revived in the twentieth century; certainly neophyte torts students today seem most reluctant to accept the notion that even a few automobile collisions can be fairly regarded as unavoidable. Somebody, they seem to think, must have been at fault.

In early common law, it has been suggested, conduct was judged more by results than by intentions. But that is not to say that it was judged by a standard that disregarded fault in favor of causation. Probably it is nearer the mark to say that conduct causing harm was considered morally blameworthy, and that close adherence to moral blameworthiness may have been sacrificed to gain supposed advantages of objective standards of judgment. Such a sacrifice may seem sensible to enlightened men—to a generation such as ours, if you please—as well as to those living far away in time or perhaps even in geographical or social setting, whom we choose to call primitive. We are uneasy about our concepts of moral responsibility.[9] And it is the more likely still that the sacrifice will be made when a society is distrustful of the capacity of its adjudicators (whether judges, juries, or others) to make the finer discriminations required in the application of a subjective standard—that is, a standard depending on the personal characteristics and the state of mind of the one being judged.

Tort law provides many illustrations of the use of relatively mechanical rules even though a more personalized standard of judgment

accident" came to be recognized as a ground for escaping liability. Bohlen, "Liability in Tort of Infants and Insane Persons," 23 *Mich. L. Rev.* 9, 14 (1924). But the lack of any intimation in the report that this idea was an innovation in 1616 suggests that it was commonly assumed before being stated in *Weaver v. Ward.* The statement, "but he ought to say that he could not do it any other way, or that he did everything that was in him to keep them out, etc., or otherwise he shall pay damages," appears as early as The Case of the Thorns, Y.B. 6 Ed. IV, f. 7, pl. 18 (1466).

Arguing that there has never been a time since the early 1500's when a defendant in trespass was not allowed to appeal to some standard of blame or fault, Wigmore observes that even "up to the 1800s we find court and counsel constantly interchanging 'inevitable accident' and 'absence of negligence or blame'" ("Responsibility for Tortious Acts," pp. 441, 444).

[9] Compare Jaffe, "Damages for Personal Injury: The Impact of Insurance," 18 *Law & Contemp. Prob.* 219, 220 (1953): "Whether fault is an effect of free will is a question that each decides for himself, but the law, following the common instinct, treats fault as a moral dictum . . . There is, however, no denying that for most of us the question of the individual's moral responsibility for fault arouses deep and discomforting metaphysical distress. The modern man is thus driven to avoid where possible solutions that invoke the concept of fault."

would commend itself if it were considered administrable. The objectively oriented standard of negligence is an important example. Also, the difficulties of making a personalized judgment of the plaintiff's harm and its causes explain in part the past reluctance of courts to extend liability in cases of emotional injury. One factor in the current trend of expanding liability for emotional injury is increasing confidence in factfinding as relatively more reliable expert evidence becomes available.

Many current trends toward broader liability represent no deviation from the theme of fault but rather a movement toward closer adherence to it. Broader liabilities for emotional injury,[10] for failure to benefit one in peril,[11] and for failure as an occupier to make one's premises safe for others [12] are examples, as is the trend toward narrowing or eliminating immunities enjoyed by charities, units of government, and persons in family relations. Another example is the trend toward comparative negligence, which is a closer approach to distributing loss in proportion to fault than the older decisional rule that contributory negligence is a complete bar. The older rules in all these instances illustrate the failure of tort law to carry through its theme of fault; they are deviations toward a narrower scope of liability than the theme of fault would support. The trend toward broader liability in all these cases may be viewed as a movement toward a finer tailoring of tort law to fault, rather than a challenge to fault as the basis of liability.

In addition to its theme of fault, tort law, as noted before, has had another distinctive feature. According to the legal tradition passed into the twentieth century, the dichotomy of shifting a loss from the plaintiff to the defendant or leaving it upon the plaintiff, where it had fallen, exhausted the field of relevant possibilities. Other possibilities that we observe today were simply not recognized. Thus the criteria for liability in tort at the beginning of the century represented the distillation of community wisdom and prejudice about reasons, good and bad, for

[10] Harper and James, *Torts,* vol. I, § § 9.1–9.7, pp. 665–691, and vol. II, § 18.4, pp. 1031–1039; Prosser, *Torts* (3rd ed. 1964), § 11, pp. 41–54, § 55, pp. 346–354.

[11] See Harper and James, *Torts,* vol. II, § 18.6, pp. 1044–1053; Prosser, *Torts* (3rd ed. 1964), § 54, pp. 336–339.

[12] Harper and James, *Torts,* vol. II, §§ 27.1–27.21, pp. 1430–1533; Prosser, *Torts* (3rd ed. 1964), §§ 57–63, pp. 358–425. In England, the Occupiers' Liability Act, 1957, 5 & 6 Eliz. 2, ch. 31, does away with the rules under which the liability of the occupier differs according to whether the visitor is an invitee or a licensee; § 2 provides instead that the occupier owes "the common duty of care" to all his lawful visitors, "except in so far as he is free to and does extend, restrict, modify or exclude his duty to any visitor or visitors by agreement or otherwise."

making one person pay another for loss suffered. In this setting, negligence was the most generally acceptable reason for legal liability. It might be that some other basis for awards could have served as well, or even better, to compensate for losses suffered, but the aim was justice as well as compensation. The prevailing thought was that this dual objective was best served by a brace of rules—first, that those who carelessly cause injuries should be liable to pay compensation to their victims and, second, that those who are unintentionally injured by nonnegligent conduct should not be compensated under tort law.

One wonders that so little appears in the literature of the law in reasoned answer to the question why the negligence principle was considered ideally fair and just. Was the principle so deeply entrenched that no one even questioned it? Or if some few wondered, did they see so little to be gained by the inquiry that thoughtful speculation seemed idle? Was there an uneasy sense that one could offer no reasoned proof that the negligence principle is just, or that it is unjust? Or did this principle so clearly conform to a community consensus about justice that the consensus itself, whatever its sources, was reason enough to sustain the principle?

Even in the writings of recent decades, as the negligence principle has come under sharp and sharper challenge, support for basing liability on negligence is traced primarily to a sense of what is just and fair, and is explained not as a conclusion reasoned from other premises, but as a perception consistent with prevailing values. Thus the best justification offered is an asserted empiric observation—that most people believe fairness requires that one who carelessly causes harm to another pay for it, and that one who unintentionally causes injury without carelessness be free of legal responsibility.

Arguably it is characteristic of human nature, even apart from the influence existing law has on attitudes, that an innocent victim feels a sense of grievance against another who negligently injures him. Unless the law provides some orderly means of satisfying the grievance, the victim and his sympathizers are likely to seek redress by antisocial methods. Thus appeasement of the offended helps to prevent further loss both to the individuals involved and to society. Negligence law serves this function of appeasement by enabling the victim to secure legal relief. Often it happens that the mere entitlement to recovery is sufficient even without its fulfillment. One who might otherwise wish to seek revenge against another who injured him slightly may choose to forego redress, satisfied by the knowledge that the law allows him relief if he wishes to take the trouble to secure it.

Negligence law may serve to prevent loss in a second way through its impact on risk-creating action. That is, it may serve to deter dangerous conduct.

Imposing liability for negligently caused injuries can contribute to long-range, general deterrence of dangerous conduct by affixing a special cost to conducting an activity or enterprise in a way that is unduly risky. This cost—either in directly discharging claims for damages or in paying premiums for liability insurance to cover such claims—can be affected substantially by the extent to which one gives attention to avoiding risk. In this way negligence law creates an incentive for loss prevention. It capitalizes on one of the most potent influences on human behavior—economic motivation.[13]

Basing liability on negligence can serve, too, as a deterrent to conduct producing undue risks of immediate harm, such as careless driving. The impact and the threat of liability based on negligence may affect driving habits also; it may have a reformative influence. As one traces its possible influence in this way he sees that there is a borderland in which long-range, general deterrence and immediate, specific deterrence merge.

All along the spectrum from the most general to the most specific deterrent influences of negligence law, adjudications of negligence can have psychological and educational effects. Placing the mark of legal disapproval, with all its practical consequences, on identifiable types of conduct may influence the attitudes and future behavior of those whose conduct is condemned. It may influence others as well, if knowledge and understanding of the adjudications can be spread through the community.

Thus far this discussion has focused on the loss-preventive function of liability based on negligence, without distinguishing between the impact of liability itself and the impact of basing it on negligence.

To what extent is appeasement accomplished because rights to com-

---

[13] Compare Calabresi, "The Decision for Accidents: An Approach to Nonfault Allocation of Costs," 78 *Harv. L. Rev.* 713, 733–737, 742–745 (1965), emphasizing the relation between general deterrence and market choices about an activity that take into account its potential for accidents.

pensation are based on negligence rather than merely because they are recognized as enforceable rights? For example, would appeasement of the innocent victim of a negligent driver be any less effective if the victim were entitled to the same compensation but on a basis of strict liability, or on a basis of loss insurance? As with the question whether a community sense of justice demands that negligent actors compensate innocent victims, here again no answer can be proved correct. Instead we must speculate. Perhaps the more persuasive speculation is that merely recognizing a right to compensation does far more to appease the offended than basing that right on negligence instead of some other theory. Indeed, in some situations persons injured through the risky but prudent activities of another have a deep sense of grievance that negligence law aggravates rather than appeases. Injuries to employees in the scope of employment can be seen in this light, and no doubt this is one reason workmen's compensation laws make employers or their insurers legally responsible for employee injuries without regard to negligence.

A similar question may be raised with respect to long-range, general deterrence of risky conduct through negligence law. How much would be lost or gained in general deterrence if liability were imposed on some broader theory of strict liability that encompassed areas of prudently risky conduct as well as unreasonably risky conduct? If the defense of contributory fault were reduced or abandoned? Again the answers must be speculative. Yet it seems likely that in this respect negligence law serves no better than carefully designed rules of strict liability might serve, and perhaps not as well.

An appropriate context in which to evaluate the effectiveness of negligence law as a specific deterrent is that area of torts most frequently litigated today—claims of traffic victims. Whenever a deviation from principles of negligence law is proposed for these injuries, champions of the status quo argue that abandoning negligence as the basis of liability would strike at the ethical foundation of tort law and destroy its inherent incentives to safety and deterrence. How well does this argument stand up under close examination?

If negligence law is to be effective in deterring dangerous driving, motorists must be able to understand what practices are condemned. Also, they must be capable of avoiding the condemned practices if they try. Negligence standards applied in these cases, however, tend to be indefinite and elastic, allowing juries to stretch one way or the other to make awards to injured plaintiffs, believing the awards will be paid by insurance companies anyway.[14]

Moreover, there has been a continuing tendency to brand as negligent more and more conduct that is neither avoidable nor morally culpable. When a defendant suffers indirectly because his insurer pays a claim against him, or even on those rare occasions when he suffers directly by paying the claim himself, he is more likely to feel aggrieved or unlucky than to feel justly chastised for misbehavior. Under these circumstances it seems doubtful indeed that standards of negligence currently applied to claims of traffic victims can have a substantial impact by way of specific deterrence.

Any possibility for such impact is further diminished by three more factors. First, many accidents are accidents in a deeper sense than negligence law recognizes—that is, they result from momentary lapses by drivers who are generally as careful as most. Second, the deterrent effect of possible legal liability is minute in comparison with other deterrents such as fear of injury to oneself or one's family or friends, fear of criminal sanctions, and fear of losing one's license to drive. Third, the virtual hopelessness of using negligence rules as deterrents is demonstrated by the difficulty of getting any driver to admit to dangerous driving—whether he is discussing his general habits or his performance on some specific occasion. Thus the attempt to use negligence law as a substantially effective deterrent to dangerous practices—as a substantial incentive to safety—founders on the fact of human psychology that more often than not the person engaging in what others regard as a dangerous practice can never be brought to believe it of himself.

If one can believe, in the face of all these reasons for doubt, that as a deterrent negligence law is substantially superior to alternative bases of liability, he must still face the fact that tort judgments are now more often paid by liability insurers than by tortfeasors. The disciple of the negligence principle might respond that secondary consequences such as higher insurance rates can still deter. But higher rates could be assessed for negligent conduct even if liability for compensation did not

---

[14] See Keeton and O'Connell, *Basic Protection for the Traffic Victim* (1965), pp. 248–249. I gratefully acknowledge that the views expressed in this and the next four paragraphs were developed in collaboration with Professor Jeffrey O'Connell, as we proceeded with the study of traffic claims on which *Basic Protection* is based. I acknowledge too the general influence of that collaborative effort on the present chapter to a greater extent than it is possible to identify specifically.

depend on negligence. And liability insurance itself seriously undercuts the supposed deterrent effect of judgments because it shelters tort-feasors from the very economic consequences that are supposed to be the principal deterrent.

Efforts to defend negligence law as serving objectives of appeasement or deterrence are, then, speculative at best and, if persuasive to any degree at all, show only a marginal utility that cannot count heavily in a calculus of reasoned choice. The main support for a continued role for negligence in the law of torts is its alleged capacity to fulfill community notions of justice. To ask whether there is a place for negligence in modern tort law is to question the status of this perceived principle of fairness. There is no shortage of eloquent affirmations supporting it. A key difficulty in appraising their validity is uncertainty about the extent to which current attitudes, rather than reflecting a deep-seated ethical commitment to the principle, reflect merely its presence in existing law. Whatever the answer to this enigma may be, it seems clear that we shall not soon exorcise the concept of negligence from the interrelated legal and ethical thought of our community.

THE SOCIAL WELFARE OBJECTIVE

When the question is asked, in its broadest form, how might our society best provide for injured persons, the range of possibilities explored must include not only liability systems—whether based on negligence or other principles—but also welfare systems of various types. Once a society has recognized as one of its objectives that its members should be provided a certain minimum level of economic welfare, then it is apparent that some accident victims are among those for whom economic benefits should be provided. The reason is not that they are accident victims, but that they are needy.

In considering the objectives of a liability system—whether based on negligence or some different principle—one is examining the utility and feasibility of recognizing obligations of compensation among individuals or other legal entities in society. What purposes are served, and at what cost, by requiring one individual or other legal entity to compensate for harm suffered by another?

In contrast, when considering the objective of social welfare, one is examining the utility and feasibility of recognizing an obligation of the society to provide a minimum standard of economic welfare for its individual members. What purposes are served, and at what cost, by providing some public fund or other mechanism for insuring that each member of the society have the benefit of the chosen minimum standard of welfare?

Perhaps every society has given at least some degree of recognition to the welfare objective. Without doubt, however, and particularly in comparison with nineteenth century states, twentieth century states have chosen a measurably increased concern with this objective.

It is in this setting that sharp debate over automobile claims systems has developed. The challenges to negligence law have not been limited to proposals for other systems of liability. They have extended, as well, to proposals for either complete or partial displacement of liability systems—whether based on negligence or other principles—by a welfare system.

This is not to say that proponents of a welfare system would disregard all objectives other than the welfare objective. Not even a system based so heavily on the welfare objective as justifiably to be called a welfare system is likely to have no regard for other objectives. For example, designers of typical welfare systems build in various inducements to deter a person, insofar as he has control over his own fate, from allowing himself to come within the group entitled to welfare benefits. Inducements are also included to encourage a person to remove himself from the welfare group promptly. It may be, too, that other objectives yet to be examined can have a part in a system that still emphasizes the welfare objective enough to warrant calling it a welfare system. For example, allocating fairly the costs of accidents may be recognized as a subsidiary objective supporting an arrangement for financing a welfare fund in part by a tax on motoring.[15]

If one took fulfillment of the welfare objective as his exclusive criterion for grading the performance of the negligence liability system as a way of compensating for injuries suffered in traffic accidents, he would give the system a very low mark indeed. He would gauge the negligence system to be inefficient—not just because of its expenditures on inquiries into fault, but also because of the costs committed to administering any system of individual liabilities.

He would gauge it to be inequitable too, by this criterion of equity: that a man should be guaranteed a certain standard of economic welfare, regardless of the nature of his impairment, whether injury or ill-

---

[15] See Franklin, "Replacing the Negligence Lottery: Compensation and Selective Reimbursement," 53 *Va. L. Rev.* 774, 803–804 (1967).

ness or inferior capabilities, and regardless of the sources and causes of his impairment, inherited or acquired. By such a criterion of equity, for example, one can say the negligence system is not evenhanded—that it does not even treat like injuries alike, much less like impairments. Implicit in such a criticism is an insistence on using as the criterion of "likeness" of injuries or other impairments the "likeness" of welfare needs they cause. Criticism of the negligence system or any other liability system on this ground is only as valid as this standard for judging evenhandedness. By this criterion, not only the negligence system, but other liability systems as well, can be described as lotteries.[16] The system is a lottery among victims if the availability and amount of compensation depend at all on any factor other than welfare need. It is a lottery among defendants, too, since it undertakes to allocate costs—to assign the burden of providing funds for compensation—on some basis apart from economic welfare of defendants.

To expose these judgments that such a criterion commands is perhaps to demonstrate that the more realistic question for one in touch with current social and political values is not whether the social welfare objective will or should completely displace the negligence liability system in the foreseeable future but rather whether and to what degree it will or should do so in part—as a way of providing subsistence or sub-subsistence benefits while liability systems based on negligence or other principles provide more. Any system of liability, in seeking to do more, will be attempting to serve some objective other than the welfare objective.

OTHER OBJECTIVES OF LIABILITY SYSTEMS

A system for meeting the economic needs of injured persons need not be based exclusively on objectives served by negligence law, or exclusively on the welfare objective, or even upon a blend of these. There are still other potential objectives that might be served by a total system.

---

[16] Franklin describes both fault and strict liability systems in this way: "One is immediately struck by the spectacular legal lottery into which the fault system thrusts the plaintiff . . . Although the lottery charge applies equally to strict liability, because victims hurt by acts of God will have no tort recovery while victims of nonnegligent human activity may, the flaw is most serious in the fault part of the tort system because of its overwhelming quantitative importance in personal injury law." ("Replacing the Negligence Lottery," p. 785.)

The objective of compensating fairly for unintended losses has often been defeated by the financial irresponsibility of those on whom the law has imposed legal liability. Negligence law itself does not deal with this problem. But without changing the theory of basing awards on negligence, lawmakers can take steps to increase the likelihood that one legally responsible for negligently caused injuries will also be financially responsible. For example, every state in the nation has enacted legislation seeking in this way to improve the practical operation of the negligence system in automobile accident cases.

Minimizing loss by distributing the burden of accidents is another objective. If accidental loss remains where it falls, its impact may be increased by secondary consequences. The burden of unexpected accidental loss may be disruptive. Even when the law provides compensation for a victim, secondary consequences can still sharply increase loss if the primary loss is merely shifted from the victim to another; the latter, too, may be so insecure financially that disruption results. If, on the other hand, the primary loss is shifted to a person or other legal entity with a capacity to distribute it widely, the impact falls lightly on each individual who must bear a share, and the likelihood of secondary loss is minimized. The prime example of an entity with such loss-distributing capacity is an insurer. Another example is a business enterprise whose operations are extensive enough to permit it to distribute losses by including in the price of its products or services an amount to be used in paying for the occasional injuries they cause.

Its champions argue that the negligence principle is a fair test for deciding what persons, activities, or enterprises in society should bear the burdens of particular types of accidents. Arguments for different principles of fairness may be advanced, however. One alternative with strong appeal may be referred to for convenience as the principle of unjust enrichment, though as will become apparent this principle is broader in scope than the rules of law this phrase traditionally connotes. Under this principle, the costs of an activity, including the costs of paying for accidental losses it causes, should be borne by those who benefit from the activity and, insofar as practicable, in proportion to the benefits they realize.

Effectuating the unjust enrichment principle requires a focus not simply upon the two parties to a tort action, but upon the classes of persons they represent—classes having relevance to the type of accidental loss in issue. An illustration of this principle is the liability of a blaster on the theory of ultrahazardous activities.[17] Placing responsibility upon the blaster for accidental injuries caused without negligence, rather than leaving each blasting victim to bear the loss, tends to distribute the cost of compensating victims in proportion to benefits realized and thereby avoids the unjust enrichment that otherwise would result to the beneficiaries of the blasting. The cost of the injuries is treated as part of the cost of the construction to which the blasting contributes. The primary appeal for this kind of cost allocation, like that for negligence law, is an appeal to one's sense of fairness.

The principles of negligence and unjust enrichment are sometimes mutually reinforcing, but at other times they clash. Consider, for example, the application of these two principles to automobile accidents. Should the cost of injuries caused in traffic accidents be treated as part of the cost of driving, to be spread among motorists in relation to advantages derived from motoring rather than being spread on the basis of negligence principles?

Principles of negligence law would leave the victim of nonnegligent motoring accidents to bear his own loss. This would result incidentally from finding no sufficient reason to shift the loss to another, rather than from determining that the innocent victim deserves to bear it. Through insurance mechanisms, on the other hand, it is easily possible to allocate to motoring generally the cost of compensating for such losses. And the principle of unjust enrichment supports the conclusion that imposing this relatively slight burden on many motorists is fairer than leaving the victims of nonnegligent motoring to bear their own losses. These losses are a part of the total cost of motoring, but an unlucky few pay for them under negligence law, contrary to the principle of spreading cost in proportion to benefits.

Quite consistently with allocating the cost of nonnegligently inflicted injuries among motorists generally, one might argue that it is fair that negligent motorists bear an added cost to compensate for injuries caused by their negligence. This is a somewhat different argument from those made earlier about achieving justice by applying negligence principles. It has strong appeal if the standards for determining negligence genuinely and realistically identify morally blameworthy conduct. As the definition of negligence is broadened to include conduct not morally blameworthy, however, the argument for applying the un-

[17] For example, *Restatement, Torts,* § 519 (1938).

just enrichment principle against the totality of motorists grows stronger while that for distributing losses on the basis of negligence, as it is defined, grows weaker.[18]

Closely related to the argument that allocating costs according to the principle of unjust enrichment is fair and just, but deserving independent recognition, is the point that legal responsibility for accidental injuries can serve as a selector of socially useful activities (or enterprises, products, or services). This point is also related to general deterrence. That is, leaving one free of legal responsibility for injuries he causes tends to work against safety, while imposing legal responsibility tends to encourage accident prevention. When the costs of injuries are assigned to the activity, an increase in the price of the service or product related to the activity is likely. This provides an economic incentive and a selector separating socially useful activities, which can pay their way in society even with this added cost, from the socially undesirable activities that cause more harm than they are worth. Thus assigning legal responsibility improves opportunities for free and rational choice concerning the worth of products and activities, both from the point of view of individuals and from the point of view of society.[19]

BASES OF LIABILITY FOR UNINTENDED INJURY

An objective of imposing legal liability can be stated in terms of a principle to which homage is due in general—a proposition so broad that it does not purport to provide answers to the multitude of specific questions confronted in applying it to individual cases. A statement of competing objectives may be useful to a degree even though no chart for their reconciliation is offered. Rules for determining liability in particular cases, in contrast, must resolve the competing ideals claiming support. Perhaps what is commonly called a basis of liability is nearer to an objective than to a rule, but at least it connotes the formulation of a broad guideline to decision that resolves in a general way the conflict among different objectives served by imposing legal liability.

No other basis of liability for unintended injury has yet commanded the widespread support that negligence has received. A number of

---

[18] Keeton and O'Connell, *Basic Protection for the Traffic Victim*, pp. 258–259.
[19] See generally *ibid.*, pp. 259–260; Calabresi, "The Decision for Accidents"; Calabresi, "Some Thoughts on Risk Distribution and the Law of Torts," 70 *Yale L. J.* 499, 500–507 (1961); James, "An Evaluation of the Fault Concept," 32 *Tenn. L. Rev.* 394, 400–403 (1965); Keeton, "Conditional Fault in the Law of Torts," 72 *Harv. L. Rev.* 401, 439–440 (1959).

competing alternatives have emerged, not only inconsistent with negligence in varying degrees but also to some extent inconsistent among themselves. They include the doctrine of *Rylands v. Fletcher*,[20] the *Restatement* doctrine of ultrahazardous activities,[21] and the rapidly spreading doctrine of strict products liability.[22] Among others that might be included are the doctrine of *Vincent v. Lake Erie Transportation Co.*[23] and the doctrine applicable to keepers of wild animals.[24]

Although in the historical development of legal doctrine the process of generalization goes on simultaneously with the development of particular rules, it often happens that a considerable body of particular illustrations develops before an organizing principle encompassing them commands recognition.

It may be that most strict liabilities now recognized are illustrations of a single basis of liability—a principle that each activity is accountable for the distinctive risks it creates. Two principal lines of argument for allocating accident costs on some basis other than negligence have been noted above—the first based on a direct appeal to one's sense of fairness and the second based on economic incentives. Perhaps both are based on the idea that each activity causes distinctive risks—that it plays a distinctive role in relation to identifiable risks that arise from its relationship to other activities, with the consequence that the contribution of other activities to these risks is different. Both lines of argument, then, support a principle that whenever a risk can be identified as distinctive to an activity, harm resulting from fruition of that risk ought in general to be charged to that activity rather than to the individual who happens to be the victim.

Limiting the scope of strict liability to harm resulting from risks distinctive to the activity bears a close analogy to limiting liability for an ultrahazardous activity to the harms of which it is a legal cause. Consider, for example, the claim of a victim who, without negligence, has fallen into the path of a carefully driven truck, loaded with high explosives. Transportation of explosives is under some authorities classified as ultrahazardous, but the risks by reason of which it is so characterized concern explosion; the harm in this case was of another type, and

[20] L.R. 3 H.L. 330 (1868).
[21] For example, *Restatement, Torts,* § 519 (1938).
[22] For example, *Restatement (Second), Torts,* § 402A (1965).
[23] 109 Minn. 456, 124 N.W. 221 (1910).
[24] For example, *Restatement, Torts,* § 507 (1938).

therefore not within the scope of liability for ultrahazardous activities.[25]

The major difficulty with the principle of distinctive risk, as with others (including the negligence principle), arises in translating it into a set of specific rules for concrete cases. For example, how are the distinctive risks of an activity to be identified? In relation to this question, products liability cases present what might be regarded as an ideal context for recognizing the principle of distinctive risk. At least in those cases in which harm results from an identifiable defect in the product, it is easy to grasp the idea that the harm is the fruition of a distinctive risk of the activity of making that product, or the activity of making and marketing it. For example, the risk of harm from defects in a woodworking machine such as the Shopsmith in *Greenman v. Yuba Power Products, Inc.*,[26] when the user is not aware of the defect, is fairly to be treated as a distinctive risk of making Shopsmiths and not as a distinctive risk of using them. Similarly, one might say that the risk of harm from defective brakes in a new car being used by one not aware of the defect is fairly to be treated as a distinctive risk of making new cars and not as a distinctive risk of using them. These risks are not to be ascribed to the activity of use, as distinguished from that of making, because the defect arises during the making even though its fruition in harm comes about only during use.

There is a sharp contrast between products liability cases and, for example, grade-crossing collision cases. Such collisions result from the interaction of two activities—motoring and railroading—and the risk of grade-crossing collisions cannot so readily be treated as a distinctive risk of either activity. This is not to say that the principle of distinctive risk can have no application to grade-crossing cases or other automobile and railroad accident cases, but only that the products liability cases plainly present a context far more favorable to the principle.

---

[25] Keeton, *Legal Cause in the Law of Torts* (1963), p. 105. Compare the debatable application of this idea in Madsen v. East Jordan Irrigation Co., 101 Utah 552, 125 P.2d 794 (1942).

For another analogy, see Albert A. Ehrenzweig, *Negligence without Fault* (1951), using "typicality" of the loss to the enterprise as a guideline to scope of liability. It seems likely, however, that "enterprise liability for harm typically and insurably caused" (p. 32) would be a liability of much broader scope, with much more overlapping of liabilities among enterprises, than liability based on a principle of distinctive risk.

[26] 59 Cal. 2d 57, 377 P.2d 897, 27 Cal. Rptr. 697 (1963), 13 A.L.R. 3d 1049 (1967).

Even in products liability cases, however, translating the principle of distinctive risk into rules of daily application poses difficult problems. Not all harm to which a product or its use contributes can be fairly classified as a distinctive risk of making or marketing the product. Requiring a defect, as recent cases imposing strict products liability have done,[27] is a way of dealing with this problem.

Strict liability, like negligence, may shift loss without distributing it. But to the extent that the persons or entities held liable have applicable liability insurance coverage, the practical result is to distribute the loss among the whole group paying premiums for that type of insurance. The same distribution and allocation of loss among the same group would be accomplished without a finding of liability if they had obtained loss insurance policies under which the insurers, for the same premiums, were obligated to pay the same victims the same amounts directly as insurance benefits rather than as payments discharging the insureds' liabilities to the victims.

The distinction between these two ways of distributing and allocating loss is essentially a formal distinction. It need have no practical significance at all. Practical consequences can be attached, however, either by design or by coincidence. For example, it is not uncommon that different statutes of limitation, specifying different periods of time, govern tort claims such as the strict liability claim and contract claims such as the loss insurance claim. Thus the choice between strict liabilities supplemented by liability insurance, on the one hand, and loss insurance on the other, though in essence formal, may have significant collateral consequences.

ACCOMMODATION

One can limit the objectives he considers in designing a system for meeting accident losses. In designing a negligence system, for example, he can disregard the welfare objective and objectives of assuring financial responsibility, minimizing secondary losses, and allocating accident costs fairly. Or in designing a welfare system he can disregard ideas about justice based on fault or on loss allocation, unjust enrichment, and the principle of distinctive risk. The system so designed, however, is not immune from criticism because of its failure to serve objectives outside those on which it is based. Any system for meeting losses from accidental injuries may fairly be criticized not only by cri-

[27] See above, pp. 108–112.

teria built on its own accepted objectives but also by criteria invoking objectives it rejects. Part of the full evaluation, in the latter case, is evaluation of the criteria themselves.

Ideas about the extent to which the welfare objective should prevail over or should yield to principles of liability are heavily value oriented. Yet it seems safe to say, as an observation of a community consensus, that as a practical matter no system can be acceptable now or in the foreseeable future without striking some accommodation between the welfare objective and objectives served by liability—an accommodation, that is, between welfare systems and tort law.

Accommodation must extend also, even within the liability phase of the total system, to principles of negligence law and to other principles as well, especially to the set of ideas referred to here as the principle of distinctive risk.

Negligence rules, developed to govern liabilities for accidental harm in a society primarily agrarian, have proved less apt for a society primarily industrial and highly mechanized. The risks of harm that the activities of one person or group impose upon others have sharply increased. The needs that the law of torts must serve are vastly different from those of earlier times. And perhaps at least as strikingly the choice of methods open to courts and legislatures has been vastly expanded. This has been due primarily to the large-scale development of devices for distributing risks and losses widely—devices that include liability insurance, loss insurance, and mass marketing of products at prices that can reflect the costs of accidental losses caused by the products. These devices have opened up new opportunities for assuring financial responsibility, for minimizing the secondary consequences of unintended losses, and for allocating accident costs otherwise than by simply choosing to leave them where they have fallen or to shift them to negligent actors.

In light of this combination of different needs and broader opportunities for allocating loss, there are deviations today from relentless pursuit of the negligence principle in tort law, and there will be more in the future.

Tort law, as law generally for that matter, is not always neat and orderly. This is not to say it is illogical. Its central logic is the logic that moves from premises, its objectives, that are only partly consistent, to conclusions, its rules, that serve each objective as well as may be while serving others too. The logic of the law extends not merely to the confining logic of compelled inferences, but also to the creative logic of maximizing service and minimizing disservice to multiple objectives. The central logic of law is this logic of accommodation.

Some observers have feared or hoped that the reduced role of negligence in tort law presages its virtual abandonment as a principle of decision. Some have suggested, for example, that negligence law and strict liability are fundamentally incompatible and in the long term cannot survive together. But law characteristically serves principles partly reinforcing and partly inconsistent. The evolving accommodation in tort law between the negligence principle and the principles of unjust enrichment and distinctive risk is no extraordinary phenomenon. Nor is it a sacrifice of justice to expediency. Rather, it is in the tradition of seeking justice through a prudent, sensitive, evenhanded, and socially acceptable accommodation among varied interests in society.

Appendix   Index

Appendix

Overruling Decisions of a Decade
1958–1967

*T*HIS IS a comprehensive, though not exhaustive, collection of overruling decisions handed down in tort cases by state courts of last resort in the United States during the ten-year period beginning January 1, 1958, and ending December 31, 1967. Notable overruling decisions of earlier years of the 1950's, of which there are only a few, are also included in this collection, with dates indicated.

Sporadic overruling had occurred earlier, but 1958 appears to be the year in which a distinctive and continuing tendency of greater freedom in overruling private law precedents began to be manifested. Decisions of that year included Butigan v. Yellow Cab Co., 49 Cal. 2d 652, 320 P.2d 500 (1958); Biakanja v. Irving, 49 Cal. 2d 647, 320 P.2d 16 (1958); Lyshak v. City of Detroit, 351 Mich. 230, 88 N.W. 2d 596 (1958); Collopy v. Newark Eye & Ear Infirmary, 27 N.J. 29, 141 A.2d 276 (1958); and Botta v. Brunner, 26 N.J. 82, 138 A.2d 713 (1958).

Perhaps other short spans of distinctive growth of tort law can be identified. For example, Francis H. Bohlen, writing the preface to a new edition of his casebook, expressed the view that 1925–1930 was a period in which American courts "made great strides in the development and analysis of the law of Torts" (*Cases on Torts*, 3rd ed. 1930, p. iii); see Friendly, "Reactions of a Lawyer—Newly Become Judge," 71 *Yale L. J.* 218, 235 (1961). But the period of which Bohlen spoke is no match for a period of the same length commencing in 1958.

In the compilation of this collection no effort was made to read all state court decisions for the years in question, but it is not likely that many overruling decisions would have failed to show up in the sources used.

In the first table below, cases are arranged by subject matter; in the second, by state.

TABLE 1. CASES ARRANGED BY SUBJECT MATTER

Government immunities: Scheele v. City of Anchorage, 385 P.2d 582 (Alaska 1963); Muskopf v. Corning Hosp. Dist., 55 Cal. 2d 211, 359 P.2d

457, 11 Cal. Rptr. 89 (1961), *on subsequent hearing sub nom.,* Corning Hosp. Dist. v. Superior Court, 57 Cal. 2d 488, 370 P.2d 325, 20 Cal. Rptr. 621 (1962); Hargrove v. Town of Cocoa Beach, 96 So. 2d 130 (Fla. 1957); Molitor v. Kaneland Community Unit Dist. No. 302, 18 Ill. 2d 11, 163 N.E.2d 89 (1959); *cert. denied,* 362 U.S. 968 (1960); Haney v. City of Lexington, 386 S.W.2d 738 (Ky. 1964); Myers v. Genesee County Auditor, 375 Mich. 1, 133 N.W.2d 190 (1965); Spanel v. Mounds View School Dist. No. 621, 264 Minn. 279, 118 N.W. 2d 795 (1962); Rice v. Clark County, 79 Nev. 253, 382 P.2d 605 (1963). See generally Annot., 86 A.L.R.2d 489 (1962); Annot., 60 A.L.R.2d 1198 (1958).

Charitable immunities: Darling v. Charleston Community Memorial Hosp., 33 Ill. 2d 326, 211 N.E.2d 253 (1965); *cert. denied,* 383 U.S. 946 (1966); Bell v. Presbytery of Boise, 421 P.2d 745 (Id. 1966); Mullikin v. Jewish Hosp. Ass'n, 348 S.W.2d 930 (Ky. 1961); Parker v. Port Huron Hosp., 361 Mich. 1, 105 N.W.2d 1 (1960); Myers v. Drozda, 180 Neb. 183, 14 N.W.2d 852 (1966) (new rule applies to actions after decision date and to earlier causes of action to the extent that liability insurance was in effect); Collopy v. Newark Eye & Ear Infirmary, 27 N.J. 29, 141 A.2d 276 (1958); Bing v. Thunig, 2 N.Y.2d 656, 143 N.E.2d 3, 163 N.Y.S.2d 3 (1957); Rabon v. Rowan Memorial Hosp., Inc., 152 S.E.2d 485 (N.C. 1967) (exhaustive review of the trend; action by paying patient for paralysis of arm and hand from injection into radial nerve; immunity preserved for churches, orphanages, rescue missions, transient homes for the indigent, and similar institutions that remain charities in fact; over-ruling applies only to present case and other causes of action arising after filing date of this opinion); Avellone v. St. John's Hosp., 165 Ohio St. 467, 135 N.E.2d 410 (1956); Hungerford v. Portland Sanitarium & Benevolent Ass'n, 235 Ore. 412, 384 P.2d 1009 (1963); Nolan v. Tifereth Israel Synagogue, 425 Pa. 106, 227 A.2d 675 (1967); Flagiello v. Pennsylvania Hosp., 417 Pa. 486, 208 A.2d 193 (1965); Adkins v. St. Francis Hosp., 143 S.E.2d 154 (W. Va. 1965); Kojis v. Doctors Hosp., 12 Wis. 2d 367, 107 N.W.2d 131, *modified on rehearing,* 12 Wis. 2d 367, 107 N.W.2d 292 (1961). See Sullivan v. First Presbyterian Church, 152 N.W.2d 628 (Iowa 1967) (interpreting a 1950 decision involving a paying hospital patient as having overruled the doctrine of charitable immunity more broadly as well). Compare Watkins v. Southcrest Baptist Church, 399 S.W.2d 530 (Tex. 1966), 44 *Texas L. Rev.* 1037, in which the majority affirmed an application of the doctrine of charitable immunity, but two members of the court (Calvert and Smith) voted to abolish the doctrine *instanter,* one (Walker) voted to abolish it prospectively but not retrospectively, and two (Greenhill and Steakley) gave notice that in their view the court should feel free to re-examine the doctrine when invoked in any case arising after the date of finality of this decision. See generally Annot., 69 A.L.R.2d 305 (1960); Annot., 25 A.L.R.2d 29 (1952).

Intrafamily immunities: Balts v. Balts, 273 Minn. 419, 142 N.W.2d 66 (1966) (Minnesota parent allowed to sue Minnesota child on Wisconsin accident; no precedent exactly in point, but bar's reasonable expectations prospectively overruled; holding limited to suit of parent against child, decision being reserved on cases of child against parent and spouse against spouse); Briere v. Briere, 224 A.2d 588 (N.H. 1966) (child permitted to sue father for nonbusiness negligent driving; prevalence of liability insurance noted); Thompson v. Thompson, 105 N.H. 86, 193 A.2d 439 (1963), 96 A.L.R.2d 969 (1964) (conflict of laws rule; tort committed in another state); Borst v. Borst, 41 Wash. 2d 642, 251 P.2d 149 (1952); Goller v. White, 20 Wis. 2d 402, 122 N.W.2d 193 (1963). Compare Hastings v. Hastings, 33 N.J. 247, 163 A.2d 147 (1960) (4–3 decision for adherence to challenged precedent; majority unconvinced of want of sound reason for retention of old rule); Badigian v. Badigian, 9 N.Y.2d 472, 174 N.E.2d 718, 215 N.Y.S. 2d 35 (1961) (6–1 decision for adherence to challenged precedent as the better rule on the merits). See generally Annot., 96 A.L.R. 2d 973 (1964); Annot., 43 A.L.R.2d 632 (1955).

Mental suffering: Battalla v. State, 10 N.Y.2d 237, 176 N.E.2d 729, 219 N.Y.S.2d 34 (1961); see Falzone v. Busch, 45 N.J. 559, 214 A.2d 12 (1965) (retroactively overruling a precedent of an intermediate court). See also Annot., 64 A.L.R.2d 100 (1959).

Prenatal injury: Amann v. Faidy, 415 Ill. 422, 114 N.E.2d 412 (1953); Keyes v. Construction Serv. Inc., 340 Mass. 633, 165 N.E.2d 912 (1960); Smith v. Brennan, 31 N.J. 353, 157 A.2d 497 (1960); Woods v. Lancet, 303 N.Y. 349, 102 N.E.2d 691 (1951); Sinkler v. Kneale, 401 Pa. 267, 164 A.2d 93 (1960); Sylvia v. Gobeille, 220 A.2d 222 (R.I. 1966) (malpractice action for failure to prescribe gamma globulin to pregnant mother exposed to measles; child not viable at the time, but action allowed); Leal v. C. C. Pitts Sand & Gravel, Inc., 419 S.W.2d 820 (Tex. 1967). See also Hatala v. Markiewicz, 26 Conn. Supp. 358, 224 A.2d 406 (1966) (action allowed; stillborn viable child); Kwaterski v. State Farm Mut. Auto. Ins. Co., 34 Wis. 2d 14, 148 N.W.2d 107 (1967) (action allowed; stillborn viable child). See generally Annot., 10 A.L.R.2d 639 (1950); Annot., 27 A.L.R.2d 1256 (1953).

Consortium claims: Deems v. Western Maryland Ry., 247 Md. 95, 231 A.2d 514 (1967) (either spouse's action for loss of consortium allowed, but must be joined with injured spouse's action; decision applicable to future and pending cases, but the claim of the wife plaintiff in this case was barred because she sued after husband's claim had been settled); Montgomery v. Stephan, 359 Mich. 33, 101 N.W.2d 227 (1960) (allowing wife's right of action for loss of consortium); Moran v. Quality Aluminum Casting Co., 34 Wis. 2d 542, 150 N.W.2d 137 (1967) (wife allowed to recover on condition actions be combined; opinion distinguishes this from precedents holding that a court must not overrule its previous statutory interpretation). Compare West v. City of San Diego, 54 Cal. 2d 469, 353 P.2d 929, 6 Cal. Rptr. 289 (1960) (denying husband's right of action for loss of consortium and disapproving a contrary holding of an intermediate appellate court of the state). In Dini v. Naiditch, 20 Ill. 2d 406, 170

N.E.2d 881 (1960), 86 A.L.R.2d 1184 (1962), the court allowed recovery by a wife and treated the issue as one of first impression in the supreme court of the state, though there had been a decision against recovery by an intermediate appellate court of the state. See Shepherd v. Consumers Coop. Ass'n, 384 S.W.2d 635 (Mo. 1964), saying the opinion in Novak v. Kansas City Transit, Inc., 365 S.W.2d 539 (Mo. 1963), creating a cause of action in favor of a wife, was necessarily retroactive because it was substantive and only those overruling decisions that concern procedural precedents are prospective. See also Annot., 23 A.L.R.2d 1378 (1952).

Measure of damages in death actions: Wycko v. Gnodtke, 361 Mich. 331, 105 N.W.2d 118 (1960) (dealing with provisions of a statute in a way well beyond the kind of judicial creativity urged in Chapter 1); Fussner v. Andert, 261 Minn. 347, 113 N.W.2d 355 (1961) (ruling that since the case was tried below under the law as it existed prior to this decision, plaintiff would be allowed a new trial only after filing a consent in writing to waive taxation of all costs and disbursements of the appeal); Lockhart v. Besel, 426 P.2d 605 (Wash. 1967) (reinterpretation of statute on child death in order to give effect to legislative intent that more than nominal damages be awarded). See also Clark v. Icicle Irrigation Dist., 432 P.2d 541 (Wash. 1967) (calling attention in note 8 to the fact that the court and the legislature were simultaneously reconsidering this problem and six days after the opinion in *Lockhart* was filed the governor signed a bill declaring that damages are permitted "for the loss of love and companionship of the child and for injury to or destruction of the parent-child relationship").

Interpretation of survival act provision on damage to "personal property": McDaniel v. Bullard, 34 Ill. 2d 487, 216 N.E.2d 140 (1966) (A's cause of action for loss of support by B saved when A later died from causes unrelated to the cause of B's death).

Liabilities of multiple tortfeasors contributing to an injury: Maddux v. Donaldson, 362 Mich. 425, 108 N.W.2d 33 (1961), 100 A.L.R.2d 1 (1965); Landers v. East Texas Salt Water Disposal Co., 151 Tex. 251, 248 S.W.2d 731 (1952). See generally Annot., 100 A.L.R.2d 16 (1965).

Effect of a release of an initial tortfeasor on the victim's action against a plastic surgeon for aggravation: see DeNike v. Mowery, 418 P.2d 1010 (Wash. 1966) (precedents distinguished, but the opinion says that strict adherence to precedents in analogous cases "would very probably have dictated" decision for the physician—p. 1012).

Contribution among tortfeasors: Bielski v. Schulze, 16 Wis. 2d 1, 114 N.W.2d 105 (1962) (adopting a rule of contribution according to percentages of causal negligence rather than in equal shares). See generally Annot., 60 A.L.R.2d 1366 (1958).

Effect of a release upon rights to contribution: Restifo v. McDonald, 426 Pa. 5, 230 A.2d 199 (1967) (decedent had released husband and wife, who later sued; administratrix permitted to join coplaintiff wife as additional defendant with respect to claim of her minor children on theory she was solely liable or liable for contribution).

Comparative negligence: Maki v. Frelk, 229 N.E.2d 284 (Ill. App. 2d Dist. 1967) (re-examining the problem, in conformity with directions from the Supreme Court of Illinois, and deciding for a rule of apportionment when plaintiff is less at fault than defendant); rev'd, Maki v. Frelk, 239 N.E.2d 445 (Ill. 1968) (majority concluding the problem is one for the legislature, not the courts).

Imputed contributory negligence: Patusco v. Prince Macaroni, Inc., 235 A.2d 465 (N.J. 1967) (wife entitled to recover, including damages for her medical expenses, despite husband's marital duty to provide medical care and despite contributory negligence of husband); Weber v. Stokely-Van Camp, Inc., 144 N.W.2d 540 (Minn. 1966) (servant's negligence not imputable to master to bar latter's claims as injured passenger suing other driver; holding limited to automobile cases, and retrospective effect limited to this case on appeal).

Presumptions concerning capacity of children to be contributorily negligent: Williamson v. Garland, 402 S.W.2d 80 (Ky. 1966).

Railroad company's duty with respect to hazards at grade crossings: Duffy v. Bill, 32 N.J. 278, 160 A.2d 822 (1960) (the legal rule regarding duty declared to be expanded, but the company's failure in this instance to provide extra precautions held as a matter of law not to be a violation of such duty).

Landlord's duty to persons on premises with tenant's consent: Rampone v. Wanskuck Bldgs., Inc., 227 A.2d 586 (R.I. 1967) (new rule applies to this case and others arising more than 60 days after opinion filed). See also the opinion imposing a duty of reasonable care on a landlord toward a tenant with respect to removal of snow and ice from common walkways, treating the issue as one of first impression, in Langhorne Road Apartments, Inc., v. Bisson, 207 Va. 474, 150 S.E.2d 540 (1966).

Occupier's duty to firemen: Dini v. Naiditch, 20 Ill. 2d 406, 170 N.E.2d 881 (1960). See generally Annot., 86 A.L.R.2d 1205 (1962).

Occupier's duty to trespassing children: Lyshak v. City of Detroit, 351 Mich. 230, 88 N.W.2d 596 (1958) (concurring opinion declares that the purport of the decision is to overrule a long line of cases).

Host driver's duty to guest passenger: Cohen v. Kaminetsky, 36 N.J. 276, 176 A.2d 483 (1961); McConville v. State Farm Mut. Auto. Ins. Co., 15 Wis. 2d 374, 113 N.W.2d 14 (1962). See also Macey v. Rozbicki, 18 N.Y.2d 289, 221 N.E.2d 380, 274 N.Y.S.2d 591 (1966); accident in Ontario, where guest act immunizes, involving New York residents, host having summer place across the river in Ontario where guest was visiting for ten days; New York law applied; note the opinion of Keating, J., 18 N.Y.2d at 298, 221 N.E.2d at 385, 274 N.Y.S.2d at 593, favoring overruling of the very recent decision in Dym v. Gordon, 16 N.Y.2d 120, 209 N.E.2d 792, 262 N.Y.S.2d 463 (1965).

Legal effect of conduct that might be called gross negligence: Bielski v. Schulze, 16 Wis. 2d 1, 114 N.W.2d 105 (1962).

Assumption of risk: Siragusa v. Swedish Hosp., 60 Wash. 2d 310, 373 P.2d 767 (1962); McConville v. State Farm Mut. Auto. Ins. Co., 15 Wis. 2d 374, 113 N.W.2d 14 (1962). See also Scott v. Liebman, 404 S.W.2d 288 (Tex. 1966) (majority opinion taking the position that a standard applied in a 1954 decision was "disapproved" in a 1963 decision).

Liability for nonnegligent trespass: see Randall v. Shelton, 293 S.W.2d 559 (Ky. 1956), and Jewell v. Dell, 284 S.W.2d 92 (Ky. 1955), declining to apply a rule of liability for unintended, nonnegligent intrusions on land, long referred to as the rule of the Kentucky streetcar cases.

Effect of res ipsa loquitur doctrine as presumption or inference: Simpson v. Gray Line Co., 226 Ore. 71, 358 P.2d 516 (1961).

Res ipsa loquitur in medical malpractice cases: Fehrman v. Smirl, 20 Wis. 2d 1, 21–22, 121 N.W.2d 255, 266 (1963). See also Beaudoin v. Watertown Mem. Hosp., 32 Wis. 2d 132, 145 N.W.2d 166 (1966) (severe burns to plaintiff's buttocks while she was under anaesthetic; error to grant motion for nonsuit).

Effect in tort action of violation of criminal statute: McConnell v. Herron, 240 Ore. 486, 402 P.2d 726 (1965) (adopting a view that violation "is negligence as a matter of law except that it may be excused where the party who failed to comply with the statute shows that his violation was caused by circumstances beyond his control"). But see Fechtman v. Stover, 199 N.E.2d 354 (Ind. App. 1964) (building council statute and regulations did not create civil liability of landlord to tenant's visitor in dwelling; if new civil liability is created, it should be done by elected body representing people); Gray v. Wisconsin Telephone Co., 30 Wis. 2d 237, 140 N.W.2d 203 (1966) (construing a statute prohibiting encumbrance of highways by poles and wires as not imposing strict liability on utility company for wires sagging across highway from broken stub pole; saying the question whether strict liability should be adopted for such cases "is a legislative policy matter and not one that should be imposed by the court").

Liability of bank to depositor for arrest following bank's carelessly dishonoring check: Weaver v. Bank of America Nat'l Trust & Sav. Ass'n, 59 Cal. 2d 428, 380 P.2d 644, 30 Cal. Rptr. 4 (1963).

Basic rule of legal cause in tort cases: see Dellwo v. Pearson, 259 Minn. 452, 107 N.W.2d 859 (1961) (reaffirming an old precedent from which opinions—but allegedly not judgments—had sometimes strayed, perhaps unwittingly, during intervening decades).

Scope of freedom for "seller's talk": Kabatchnick v. Hanover-Elm Bldg. Corp., 328 Mass. 341, 103 N.E.2d 692 (1952), 30 A.L.R.2d 918 (1953). This decision came five years before commencement of the decade in which the distinctive tendency of greater freedom in overruling developed. Though no overruling decision on this subject during that decade has been found, substantial changes from what the law was previously thought to be have been effected without the head-on collision with precedents that produces overruling decisions. See, for example, Obde v. Schlemeyer, 56 Wash. 2d 449, 353 P.2d 672 (1960) (duty on seller of residence to inform prospective buyer of termite infestation not readily observable on reasonable inspection).

Privity: Biakanja v. Irving, 49 Cal. 2d 647, 320 P.2d 16 (1958), 65 A.L.R.2d 1358 (1959) (suit by intended beneficiary of will against notary public responsible for its being executed with insufficient witnesses); Hamon v. Digliani, 148 Conn. 710, 174 A.2d 294 (1961) (suit by purchaser of detergent against manufacturer and retailer); McCormack v. Hankscraft Co., 154 N.W.2d 488 (Minn. 1967) (suit against manufacturer of vaporizers for injuries to child of purchaser); State Stove Mfg. Co. v. Hodges, 189 So. 2d 113 (Miss. 1966); *cert. denied,* 386 U.S. 912 (1967) (majority, however, held for manufacturer on theory the hot-water heater in question was not defective as manufactured and that intervening negligence of contractors in failing to follow installation instructions was the sole proximate cause of explosion); Henningsen v. Bloomfield Motors, Inc., 32 N.J. 358, 161 A.2d 69 (1960), 75 A.L.R.2d 1 (1961) (suit by automobile purchaser's wife against manufacturer and retailer); Faber v. Creswick, 31 N.J. 234, 156 A.2d 252 (1959) (suit by tenant's wife against landlord); Goldberg v. Kollsman Instrument Corp., 12 N.Y.2d 432, 191 N.E.2d 81, 240 N.Y.S.2d 592 (1963) (suit by air crash victim's representative against aircraft assembler and others); Greenberg v. Lorenz, 9 N.Y.2d 195, 173 N.E.2d 773, 213 N.Y.S.2d 39 (1961) (suit against retailer by child of purchaser of canned salmon); Rampone v. Wanskuck Bldgs., Inc., 227 A.2d 586 (R.I. 1967) (suit by tenant's employee against landlord); Strakos v. Gehring, 360 S.W.2d 787 (Tex. 1962) (suit against contractor for injuries suffered by third person after contractor's work had been accepted). See Lucas v. Hamm, 56 Cal. 2d 583, 364 P.2d 685, 15 Cal. Rptr. 821 (1961) (dictum in suit by intended beneficiary against attorney whose alleged negligence in drafting a will that violated the rule against perpetuities defeated the beneficiary's intended interest); Slavin v. Kay, 108 So. 2d 462 (Fla. 1959) (adopting a new theory, though without explicitly overruling any particular precedent). See generally Annot., 78 A.L.R.2d 1238 (1961); Annot., 75 A.L.R.2d 39 (1961); Annot., 58 A.L.R. 2d 865 (1958).

Strict products liability: Henningsen v. Bloomfield Motors, Inc., 32 N.J. 358, 161 A.2d 69 (1960), 75 A.L.R.2d 1 (1961). Perhaps the following cases should be regarded as overruling a body of precedents though without identifying particular cases: Greenman v. Yuba Power Prods., Inc., 59 Cal. 2d 57, 377 P.2d 897, 27 Cal. Rptr. 697 (1963), 13 A.L.R. 3d 1049 (1967); McCormack v. Hankscraft Co., 154 N.W.2d 488 (Minn. 1967); Goldberg v. Kollsman Instrument Corp., 12 N.Y.2d 432, 191 N.E.2d 81, 240 N.Y.S. 2d 592 (1963); Webb v. Zern, 422 Pa. 424, 220 A.2d 853 (1966) (majority recognize strict products liability as set forth in *Restatement (Second), Torts,* § 402A; Bell dissents, berating majority for engaging in the legislative function of overruling, and doing it without saying so); McKisson

v. Sales Affiliates, Inc., 416 S.W.2d 787 (Tex. 1967); Dippel v. Sciano, 155 N.W.2d 55 (Wis. 1967). In Shoshone Coca-Cola Bottling Co. v. Dolinski, 420 P.2d 855 (Nev. 1967), the court adopted strict liability and explicitly overruled decisions bearing on how the cause of action is to be proved. See Green v. American Tobacco Co., 391 F.2d 97 (5th Cir. 1968) (interpreting Florida law); Dealers Transport Co. v. Battery Distributing Co., 402 S.W.2d 441 (Ky. 1966) (presented as consistent with a previous overruling decision rather than a new departure). See generally Prosser, "The Fall of the Citadel," 50 *Minn. L. Rev.* 791 (1966).

Per diem arguments and related methods of advocacy: Botta v. Brunner, 26 N.J. 82, 138 A.2d 713 (1958). In Duguay v. Gelinas, 104 N.H. 182, 182 A.2d 451 (1962), the court affirmed a trial judge's refusal to allow the use of a mathematical formula or to allow counsel to place a value on component parts of the total injuries. The court was able to deal with the precise issue before it as one of first impression, though it seems likely that this decision has wrought a change in the practices occurring in the trial courts of the state. See generally Annot., 60 A.L.R.2d 1347 (1958).

Instructions on unavoidable accident: Butigan v. Yellow Cab Co., 49 Cal. 2d 652, 320 P.2d 500 (1958), 65 A.L.R.2d 1 (1959); Lewis v. Buckskin Joe's, Inc., 156 Colo. 46, 396 P.2d 933 (1964) (precedents overruled prospectively, applying to present case since new trial was granted); Graham v. Rolandson, 435 P.2d 263 (Mont. 1967) (prospective application only); Fenton v. Aleshire, 238 Ore. 24, 393 P.2d 217 (1964). See also Vespe v. DiMarco, 43 N.J. 430, 204 A.2d 874 (1964).

Implied waiver of jury trial by moving for directed verdict: Godell v. Johnson, 418 P.2d 505 (Ore. 1966).

Qualification of medical witness: Shoshone Coca-Cola Bottling Co. v. Dolinski, 420 P.2d 855 (Nev. 1967) (overruling a decision disallowing testimony when the witness had not treated the patient). See also Hundley v. Martinez, 158 S.E.2d 159 (W. Va. 1967) (disapproving a strict "locality rule" under which one would have to be familiar with standards of medical care in the community in question; reasoned, however, as an issue of first impression, an earlier decision being distinguished and limited).

Malpractice limitation statutes: Berry v. Branner, 421 P.2d 996 (Ore. 1966) (overruling a 1964 precedent, discussing effect of legislative inaction); Gaddis v. Smith, 417 S.W.2d 577 (Tex. 1967); Morgan v. Grace Hosp., Inc., 149 W. Va. 783, 144 S.E.2d 156 (1965). See Yoshizaki v. Hilo Hosp., 433 P.2d 220 (Hawaii 1967) (reversing on rehearing its original decision to the contrary in a case of first impression).

Standard for directed verdict: Pedrick v. Peoria & E. R.R., 37 Ill. 2d 494, 229 N.E.2d 504 (1967) (reasoned as a clarification of apparently conflicting standards in various precedents).

TABLE 2. CASES ARRANGED BY STATES

Alaska: Scheele v. City of Anchorage, 385 P.2d 582 (Alaska 1963).
California: Weaver v. Bank of America Nat'l Trust & Sav. Ass'n, 59 Cal.

2d 428, 380 P.2d 644, 30 Cal. Rptr. 4 (1963); Greenman v. Yuba Power Prods., Inc., 59 Cal. 2d 57, 377 P.2d 897, 27 Cal. Rptr. 697 (1963), 13 A.L.R.3d 1049 (1967); Muskopf v. Corning Hosp. Dist., 55 Cal. 2d 211, 359 P.2d 457, 11 Cal. Rptr. 89 (1961), *on subsequent hearing sub nom.*, Corning Hosp. Dist. v. Superior Court, 57 Cal. 2d 488, 370 P.2d 325, 20 Cal. Rptr. 621 (1962); Butigan v. Yellow Cab Co., 49 Cal. 2d 652, 320 P.2d 500 (1958), 65 A.L.R.2d 1 (1959); Biakanja v. Irving, 49 Cal. 2d 647, 320 P.2d 16 (1958), 65 A.L.R.2d 1358 (1959).

Colorado: Lewis v. Buckskin Joe's, Inc., 156 Colo. 46, 396 P.2d 933 (1964).

Connecticut: Hamon v. Digliani, 148 Conn. 710, 174 A.2d 294 (1961).

Florida: Hargrove v. Town of Cocoa Beach, 96 So. 2d 130 (Fla. 1957).

Hawaii: Yoshizaki v. Hilo Hosp., 433 P.2d 220 (Hawaii 1967).

Idaho: Bell v. Presbytery of Boise, 421 P.2d 745 (Id. 1966).

Illinois: Pedrick v. Peoria & E. R.R., 37 Ill. 2d 494, 229 N.E.2d 504 (1967); McDaniel v. Bullard, 34 Ill. 2d 487, 216 N.E.2d 140 (1966); Darling v. Charleston Community Memorial Hosp., 33 Ill. 2d 326, 211 N.E.2d 253 (1965); Dini v. Naiditch, 20 Ill. 2d 406, 170 N.E.2d 881 (1960), 86 A.L.R.2d 1184 (1962); Molitor v. Kaneland Community Unit Dist. No. 302, 18 Ill. 2d 11, 163 N.E.2d 89 (1959), *cert. denied,* 362 U.S. 968 (1960); Amann v. Faidy, 415 Ill. 422, 114 N.E.2d 412 (1953). See also Maki v. Frelk, 229 N.E.2d 284 (Ill. App. 2d Dist. 1967); rev'd Maki v. Frelk, 239 N.E.2d 445 (Ill. 1968).

Iowa: Sullivan v. First Presbyterian Church, 152 N.W.2d 628 (Iowa 1967), adhering to and interpreting broadly the overruling decision in Haynes v. Presbyterian Hosp. Ass'n, 241 Iowa 1269, 45 N.W.2d 151 (1950).

Kentucky: Williamson v. Garland, 402 S.W.2d 80 (Ky. 1966); Haney v. City of Lexington, 386 S.W.2d 738 (Ky. 1964); Mullikin v. Jewish Hosp. Ass'n, 348 S.W.2d 930 (Ky. 1961); Randall v. Shelton, 293 S.W.2d 559 (Ky. 1956); Jewell v. Dell, 284 S.W.2d 92 (Ky. 1955). See also City of Louisville v. Chapman, 415 S.W.2d 74 Ky. 1967) (adhering to *Haney*).

Maryland: Deems v. Western Maryland Ry., 247 Md. 95, 231 A.2d 514 (1967).

Massachusetts: Keyes v. Construction Serv. Inc., 340 Mass. 633, 165 N.E.2d 912 (1960); Kabatchnick v. Hanover-Elm Bldg. Corp., 328 Mass. 341, 103 N.E.2d 692 (1952), 30 A.L.R.2d 918 (1953).

Michigan: Myers v. Genesee County Auditor, 375 Mich. 1, 133 N.W.2d 190 (1965); Maddux v. Donaldson, 362 Mich. 425, 108 N.W.2d 33 (1961), 100 A.L.R.2d 1 (1965); Wycko v. Gnodtke, 361 Mich. 331, 105 N.W.2d 118 (1960); Parker v. Port Huron Hosp., 361 Mich. 1, 105 N.W.2d 1 (1960); Montgomery v. Stephan, 359 Mich. 33, 101 N.W.2d 227 (1960); Lyshak v. City of Detroit, 351 Mich. 230, 88 N.W.2d 596 (1958).

Minnesota: McCormack v. Hankscraft Co., 154 N.W.2d 488 (Minn. 1967); Weber v. Stokeley-Van Camp, Inc., 144 N.W.2d 540 (Minn. 1966); Balts v. Balts, 273 Minn. 419, 142 N.W.2d 66 (1966); Spanel v. Mounds View School Dist. No. 621, 264 Minn. 279, 118 N.W.2d 795 (1962); Fussner v. Andert, 261 Minn. 347, 113 N.W.2d 355 (1961); Dellwo v. Pearson, 259 Minn. 452, 107 N.W.2d 859 (1961).

Mississippi: State Stove Mfg. Co. v. Hodges, 189 So.2d 113 (Miss. 1966).

Montana: Graham v. Rolandson, 435 P.2d 263 (Mont. 1967).

Nebraska: Myers v. Drozda, 180 Neb. 183, 141 N.W.2d 852 (1966).

Nevada: Shoshone Coca-Cola Bottling Co. v. Dolinski, 420 P.2d 855 (Nev. 1967); Rice v. Clark County, 79 Nev. 253, 382 P.2d 605 (1963).

New Hampshire: Briere v. Briere, 224 A.2d 588 (N.H. 1966); Thompson v. Thompson, 105 N.H. 86, 193 A.2d 439 (1963), 96 A.L.R.2d 969 (1964). See also Duguay v. Gelinas, 104 N.H. 182, 182 A.2d 451 (1962).

New Jersey: Patusco v. Prince Macaroni, Inc., 235 A.2d 465 (N.J. 1967); Cohen v. Kaminetsky, 36 N.J. 276, 176 A.2d 483 (1961); Henningsen v. Bloomfield Motors, Inc., 32 N.J. 358, 161 A.2d 69 (1960), 75 A.L.R.2d 1 (1961); Duffy v. Bill, 32 N.J. 278, 160 A.2d 822 (1960); Smith v. Brennan, 31 N.J. 353, 157 A.2d 497 (1960); Faber v. Creswick, 31 N.J. 234, 156 A.2d 252 (1959); Collopy v. Newark Eye & Ear Infirmary, 27 N.J. 29, 141 A.2d 276 (1958); Botta v. Brunner, 26 N.J. 82, 138 A.2d 713 (1958). See also Falzone v. Busch, 45 N.J. 559, 214 A.2d 12 (1965).

New York: Goldberg v. Kollsman Instrument Corp., 12 N.Y.2d 432, 191 N.E.2d 81, 240 N.Y.S.2d 592 (1963); Battalla v. State, 10 N.Y.2d 237, 176 N.E.2d 729, 219 N.Y.S.2d 34 (1961); Greenberg v. Lorenz, 9 N.Y.2d 195, 173 N.E.2d 773, 213 N.Y.S.2d 39 (1961); Bing v. Thunig, 2 N.Y.2d 656, 143 N.E.2d 3, 163 N.Y.S.2d 3 (1957); Woods v. Lancet, 303 N.Y. 349, 102 N.E.2d 691 (1951).

North Carolina: Rabon v. Rowan Mem. Hosp., Inc., 152 S.E.2d 485 (N.C. 1967).

Ohio: Avellone v. St. John's Hosp., 165 Ohio St. 467, 135 N.E.2d 410 (1956).

Oregon: Berry v. Branner, 421 P.2d 996 (Ore. 1966); Godell v. Johnson, 418 P.2d 505 (Ore. 1966); McConnell v. Herron, 240 Ore. 486, 402 P.2d 726 (1965); Fenton v. Aleshire, 238 Ore. 24, 393 P.2d 217 (1964); Hungerford v. Portland Sanitarium & Benevolent Ass'n, 235 Ore. 412, 384 P.2d 1009 (1963); Simpson v. Gray Line Co., 226 Ore. 71, 358 P.2d 516 (1961).

Pennsylvania: Restifo v. McDonald, 426 Pa. 5, 230 A.2d 199 (1967); Nolan v. Tifereth Israel Synagogue, 425 Pa. 106, 227 A.2d 675 (1967); Flagiello v. Pennsylvania Hosp., 417 Pa. 486, 208 A.2d 193 (1965); Sinkler v. Kneale, 401 Pa. 267, 164 A.2d 93 (1960). See also Webb v. Zern, 422 Pa. 424, 220 A.2d 853 (1966).

Rhode Island: Rampone v. Wanskuck Bldgs., Inc., 227 A.2d 586 (R.I. 1967); Sylvia v. Gobeille, 220 A.2d 222 (R.I. 1966).

Texas: Leal v. C. C. Pitts Sand & Gravel, Inc., 419 S.W.2d 820 (Tex. 1967); Gaddis v. Smith, 417 S.W.2d 577 (Tex. 1967); Strakos v. Gehring, 360 S.W.2d 787 (Tex. 1962); Landers v. East Texas Salt Water Disposal Co., 151 Tex. 251, 248 S.W.2d 731 (1952). See McKisson v. Sales Affiliates, Inc., 416 S.W.2d 787 (Tex. 1967) (expanding strict products liability beyond products intended for human consumption but without overruling any specific precedents); Scott v. Liebman, 404 S.W.2d 288 (Tex. 1966) (taking the position that a 1963 decision had "disapproved" a 1954 decision). See also the dissenting and concurring opinions in Watkins v. Southcrest Baptist Church, 399 S.W.2d 530 (Tex. 1966).

Washington: Lockhart v. Besel, 426 P.2d 605 (Wash. 1967); DeNike v. Mowery, 418 P.2d 1010 (Wash. 1966); Siragusa v. Swedish Hosp., 60 Wash. 2d 310, 373 P.2d 767 (1962); Borst v. Borst, 41 Wash. 2d 642, 251 P.2d 149 (1952).

West Virginia: Morgan v. Grace Hosp., Inc., 149 W. Va. 783, 144 S.E.2d 156 (1965); Adkins v. St. Francis Hosp., 143 S.E.2d 154 (W. Va. 1965).

Wisconsin: Dippel v. Sciano, 155 N.W.2d 55 (Wis. 1967); Moran v. Quality Aluminum Casting Co., 34 Wis. 2d 542, 150 N.W.2d 137 (1967); Fehrman v. Smirl, 20 Wis. 2d 1, 22, 121 N.W.2d 255, 266 (1963); Goller v. White, 20 Wis. 2d 402, 122 N.W.2d 193 (1963); Bielski v. Schulze, 16 Wis. 2d 1, 114 N.W.2d 105 (1962); McConville v. State Farm Mut. Auto. Ins. Co., 15 Wis. 2d 374, 113 N.W.2d 14 (1962); Kojis v. Doctors Hosp., 12 Wis. 2d 367, 107 N.W.2d 131, *modified on rehearing,* 107 N.W.2d 292 (1961).

Index

Date Due
